ALTERNATE TUNINGS

PICTURE CHORDS

By Mark Hanson

Published by:

ACCENT ON MUSIC
19363 Willamette Dr. #252
West Linn, OR 97068 USA

First Printing 1997 10 9 8 7 6 5 4 3 2 1
Printed in the United States of America.

Library of Congress Catalogue in Publication Data
Hanson, Mark D. 1951-
Alternate Tunings Picture Chords
1. Guitar—Methods—Self-Instruction. I. Title.

ISBN 0-936799-14-5 Paperback

Table Of Contents

Introduction

Welcome to *Alternate Tunings Picture Chords*! You are opening the pages to a world of information on a most elusive subject: guitar chords in alternate tunings.

Most guitarists begin their exploration of the instrument using the familiar first-position chords in standard tuning, which is E A d g b e', lowest pitch to highest. After some time, many players become intrigued with the sonorous world of alternate tunings, and the tuning machines begin to turn. But what happens when the strings are tuned to different notes? The chords you learned in standard tuning don't work anymore. Where do you start to learn the new ones? This book is the place.

The Tunings

This book is designed to be an encyclopedia of chords in non-standard tunings. You will find 1,340 chords in 56 tunings in these pages. The tunings range from the common to the unusual, covering nearly every style of music.

Many of the tunings are close to standard, like the common Drop-D (D A d g b e') and Chet Atkins' A9 tuning (E A c# g b e'), where only one string is altered from standard. But there are also tunings that require that all six strings be changed: Joni Mitchell's "Turbulent Indigo" tuning of B' F# d# d# f# b, and Martin Simpson's "Young Man" tuning of C G c f c' d', for instance.

The Chords

"How will I remember all of these chords, or even a few of them?" you ask? Thankfully, many of the chord fingerings used in these tunings are exceedingly easy--all open strings, for instance. See pages 32, 79, and 82 for examples. Nearly as easy as those are the numerous chords that require only one note to be fingered. Pages 32 and 68 provide good examples of one-finger chords.

Also, many familiar standard-tuning fingerings are used in alternate tunings. These chords will be easy to play and to remember because of the familiar fingerings, but they will provide a different sound than what they produce in standard tuning. The first chord on page 34 is a good example. This fingering produces an E7 sound in standard tuning, but in Open-D tuning the same fingering produces a beautiful Gadd9 sound. Another good example is the rich-sounding Cadd9 chord on page18. In standard tuning this fingering produces a simple C chord.

In many alternate tunings, you also will find numerous examples of first-position standard-tuning fingerings placed elsewhere on the fretboard. In Open-D tuning on page 32 , for example, you will find the following first-position standard-tuning chord formations: Dm, Amaj7, E, E7, and A7. But they all are fingered in different places on the fretboard to produce the proper sounds in Open-D tuning. A number of other notable examples occur on pages 123 and 140.

Other alternate-tuning chords require that you learn new fingerings, of course. Some also require quite a stretch in the fretting hand. See the Cmaj9 on page 18 for an example. One chord in the book even requires that you fret notes with both hands at once! You will find Michael Hedges' two-handed C/F chord on page 102.

Be aware that in some instances the same chord fingerings can be used in different tunings. This works if the intervals between strings in the different tunings are in the same order. For instance, Open-D and Open-G tunings have the same intervals between strings, but moved over one string. (The major-third interval in Open-D is between the third and fourth strings. That same interval is found between the second and third strings in Open-G.) So the chords are largely interchangeable. You simply have to move the fingerings from the first tuning one or more strings toward the treble or bass for the related tuning.

In general, chord fingerings in alternate tunings tend to be fairly easy. That's one of the main reasons people use tunings.

Interesting Chord Progressions

For each tuning in this book, chords are organized by letter names, starting with the tonic chord and progressing up the scale. In a number of tunings, the final chords comprise a particularly appealing chord progression utilizing one fingering, perhaps with slight variations. For instance, you may enjoy exploring the three chord progressions found in the final 16 chords of Open-D tuning on pages 35-36. You will find another example in the final four chords on page 45.

Experimenting with Fingerings

Any barre-chord shape in alternate tunings can be moved to another fret to produce a different chord. To determine the name of the new chord when you move the barre, you need to know which string in the fingering produces the root note. Then count up or down the neck on that string from the old position to the new one. Another method is simply to count up to the new position from the nut (the pitch of which you know from the name of the tuning), or count down from the twelfth fret (if your new chord is below the twelfth fret!).

Alternate-tuning fingerings that include open strings can be moved up and down the neck as well. Here you must be aware of the pitch of the open strings in conjunction with the new fretted notes. They may clash badly, or they may produce an attractive new harmony that you might never have discovered in standard tuning. Try moving a standard-tuning E fingering up and down the neck in Open-D tuning, for example. You will find this fingering in two positions on pages 32-33. Also experiment with an A-chord fingering in Open-Gm tuning, as shown on page 65.

Omitting Strings

Often, especially in fingerstyle playing, not all six strings of a chord fingering are picked. Experiment with the chords you are learning in this book by picking combinations of strings--two, three, four, or five at a time. This may help you pick out melodies in a tuning, while harmonizing them fairly simply, perhaps without fretting all the strings that are called for in the photograph.

Other New Tunings

Any of these tunings can be raised or lowered to other pitches, depending on what sounds good on your guitar, or to better fit the vocal range of a singer. Open-D tuning, for example, becomes Open-C tuning (C G c e g c') if all the strings are lowered one whole-step from Open-D. It becomes Open-B tuning (B' F# B d# f# b) if the strings are lowered an additional half-step. Notice that the notes of this Open-C tuning are in a different order than the Open-C tuning shown on page 79.

Because it would be impossible to include every alternate tuning in *Alternate Tunings Picture Chords*, I have covered the most popular, plus less common ones that are used by well-known artists. If you want chords for a tuning that is not included in this book, try this: find a tuning in the book that is close to the tuning you want; determine which strings are different and by how much; then, for each chord shown, move the fingers on the affected strings the proper amount up or down the string to produce the chord.

Fingerings

Well-practiced guitarists realize that there are several fingerings for most chords. The fingerings shown in the photographs in *Alternate Tunings Picture Chords* are suggestions, but if a different fingering works for you, please feel free to use it.

Keep your hands as relaxed as possible when fretting any chord. During the photography session, I often pulled non-fretting fingers away from the fretboard so that you, the viewer, would have an unencumbered view of the entire fretboard. No non-fretting fingers would be in the way. This led to some unnecessary tension in my left hand. The way I actually play some of these chords in performance would look slightly different than the photos, with non-fretting fingers in a relaxed position in front of the fretboard, ready to fret the next chord.

The Notation

As you would expect, the tunings are depicted in letter names. The use of upper and lower case letters, and added primes ('), show the different octaves of the notes. In guitar notation, a lower case letter with a prime (c', e') depicts a string tuned at middle C or above. (In standard tuning, only the treble E string on the guitar is tuned above middle C.) A lower case letter without a prime (c, e) depicts a string tuned in the octave directly below middle C. An upper case letter (C, E) depicts a string tuned between one and two octaves below middle C. An upper case letter with a prime (B') depicts a string tuned in the third octave below middle C.

The standard notation, tablature and chord grids are all included to assist you in your understanding of the chords included in the book.

In Closing

Even though *Alternate Tunings Picture Chords* contains an abundance of information, it doesn't necessarily explain how to use these tunings and chords in a musical fashion. That is left to you. To learn more about how to use alternate tunings, I highly recommend that you study my book *The Complete Book of Alternate Tunings*, which you can find in any retail music store, or order from the back of this book. It provides great insight into working with tunings. It also provides an exhaustive list of artists, and the tunings they use for their compositions.

Have a great time investigating *Alternate Tunings Picture Chords*. I hope it will bring you much pleasure and satisfaction for many years to come!

--Mark Hanson

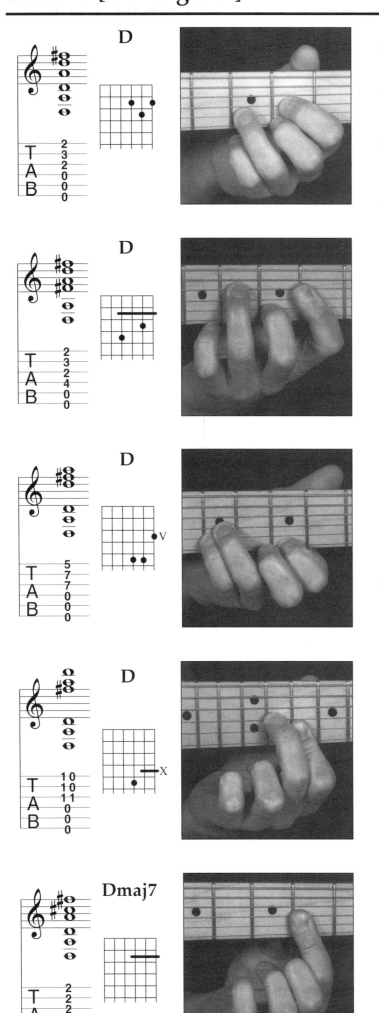

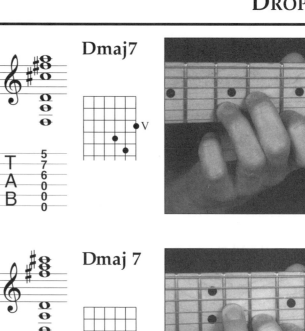

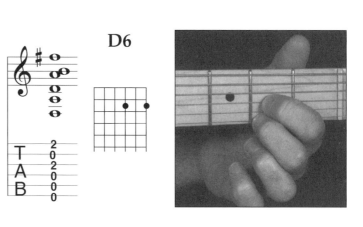

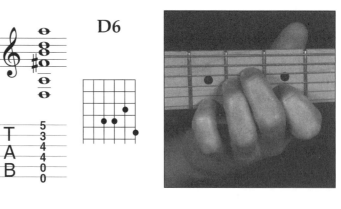

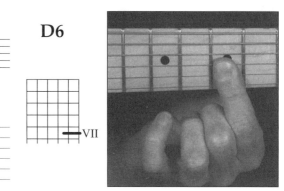

D6
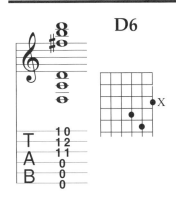
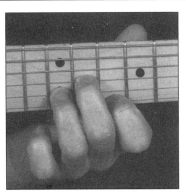

Dmaj9
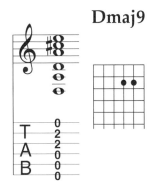

Dadd 9
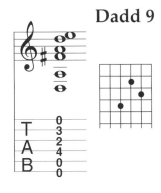
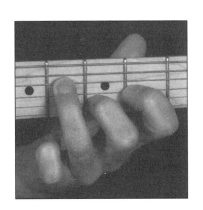

Dmaj9
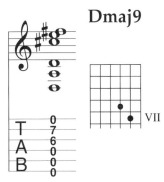
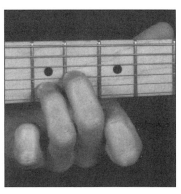

Dadd9
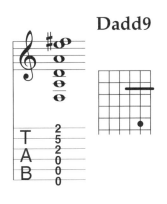
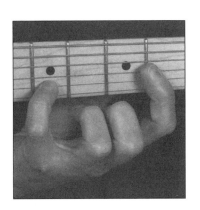

Dmaj9
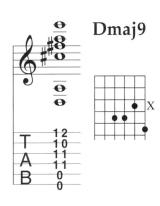

Dadd9
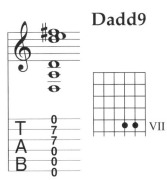
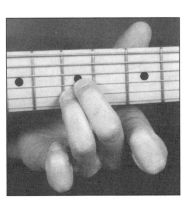

D6add9
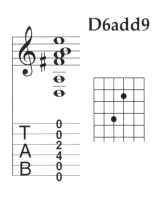

Dadd9
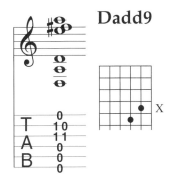

D6add9
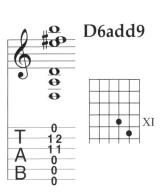
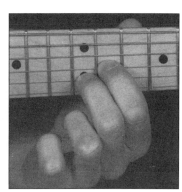

D7

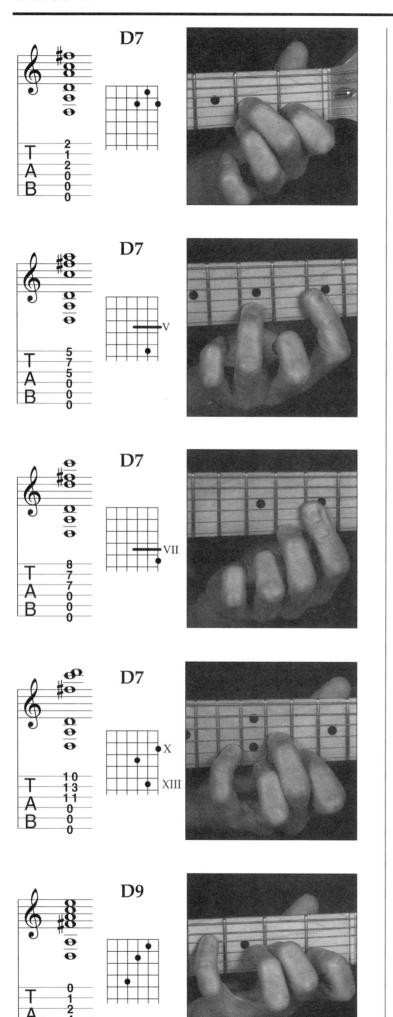

D9

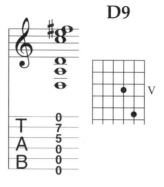

D9

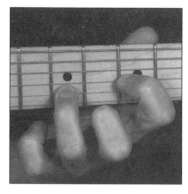

D7

D9

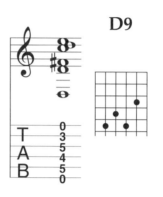

D7

D9

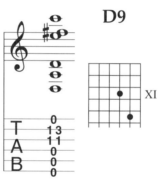
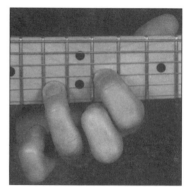

D7

D9

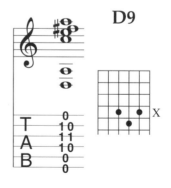

D9

D9

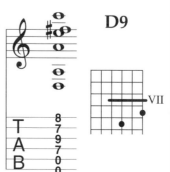
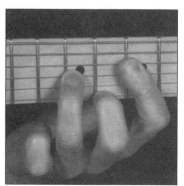

Dm

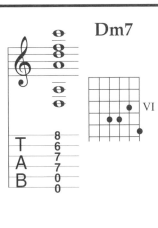

Dm

Dm

Dm7

Dm7

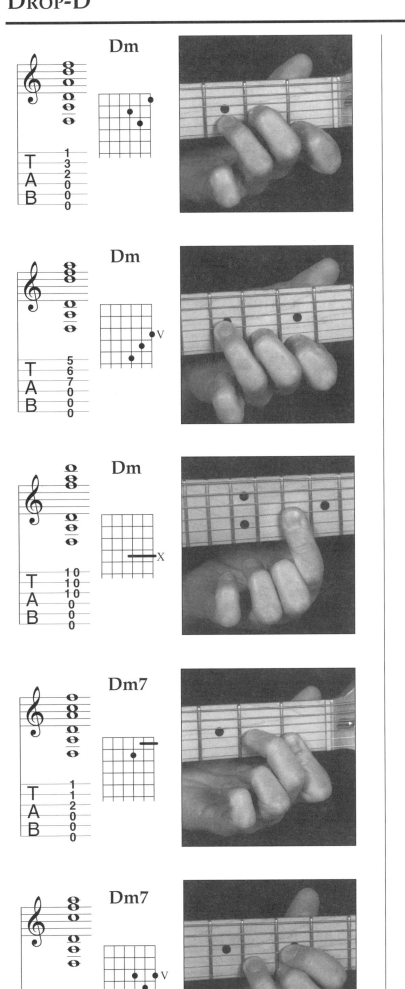

Dm7

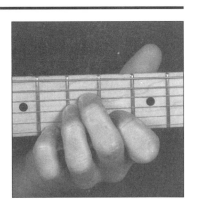

Dm7

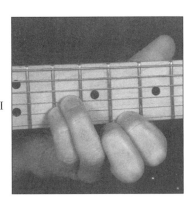

Dm6

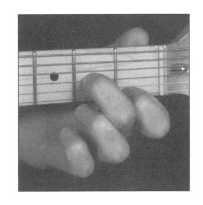

Dm6

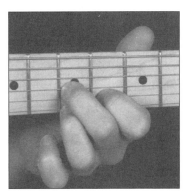

Dm6

Dm9

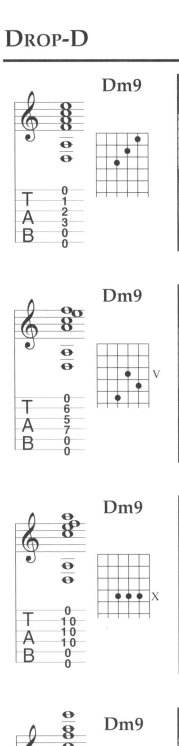
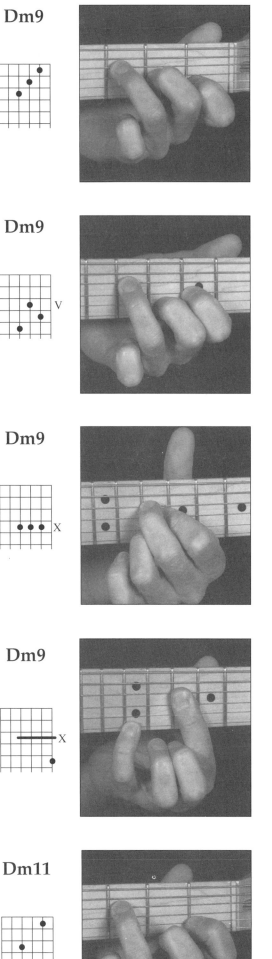

```
T  0
A  1
B  2
   3
   0
   0
```

Dm9

```
T  0
A  6
B  5
   7
   0
```

Dm9

```
T  0
A  10
B  10
   10
   0
   0
```

Dm9

```
T  12
A  10
B  10
   10
   0
   0
```

Dm11

```
T  0
A  1
B  0
   3
   0
   0
```

Dm11

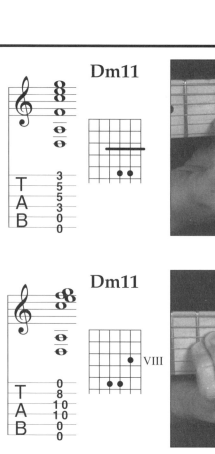

```
T  3
A  5
B  5
   3
   0
   0
```

Dm11

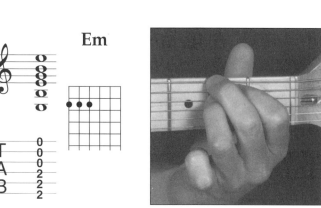

```
T  0
A  8
B  10
   10
   0
   0
```

Em

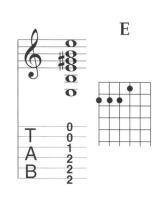

```
T  0
A  0
B  0
   2
   2
   2
```

E

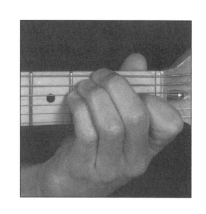

```
T  0
A  0
B  1
   2
   2
   2
```

Dm11

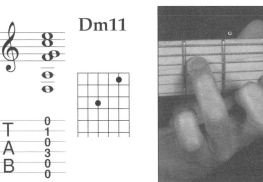

Em9

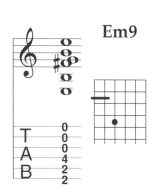
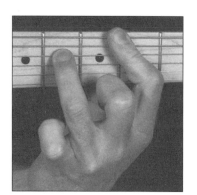

```
T  0
A  0
B  0
   4
   2
   2
```

F

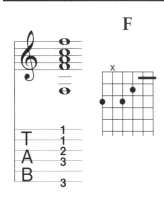
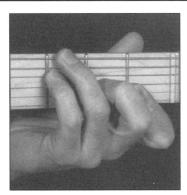

Fm7

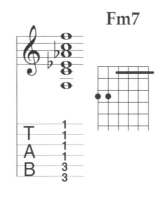
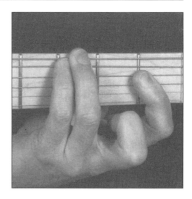

Fmaj7

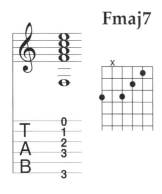

Fm

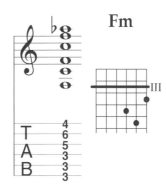
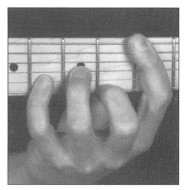

F7

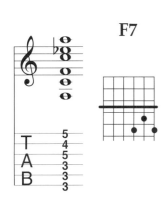
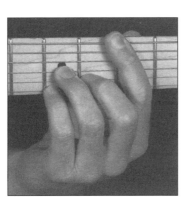

F#m

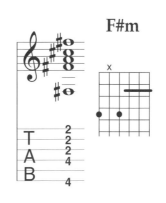
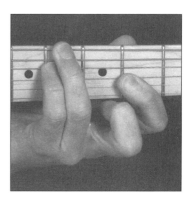

F6

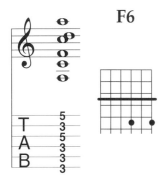
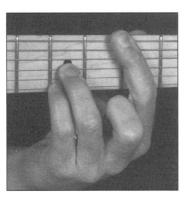

F#m7

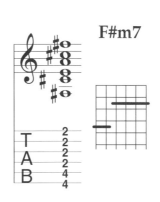
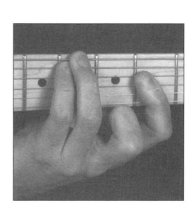

Fm

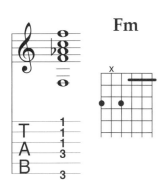
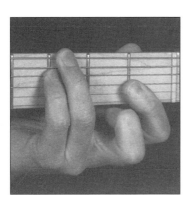

F#m7

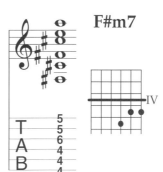

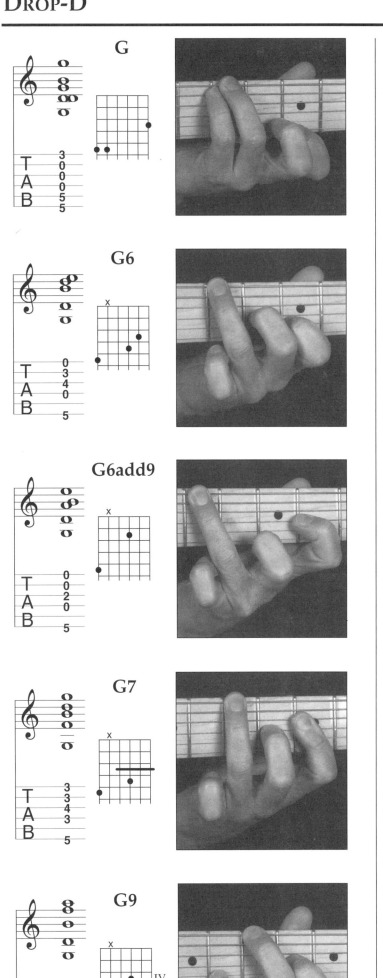

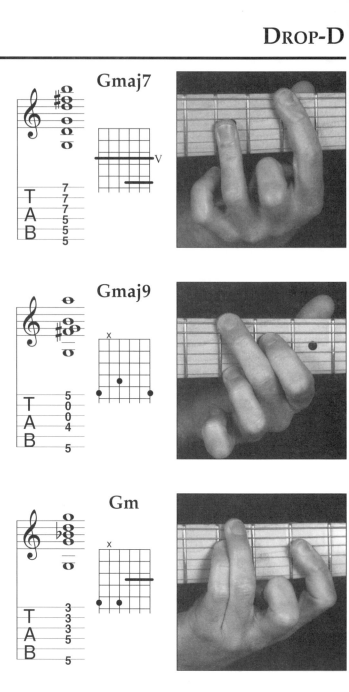

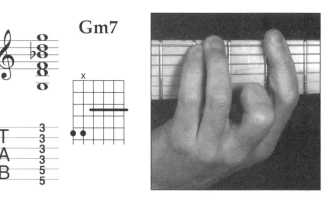

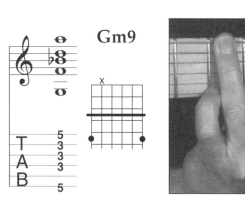

A

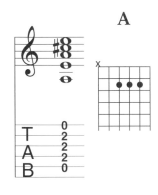
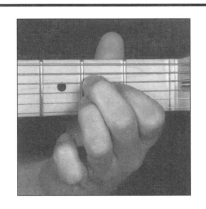

Am

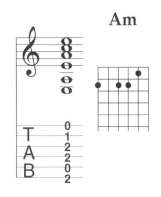

A

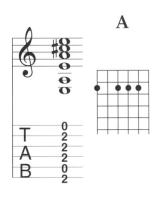
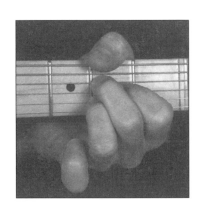

Am7

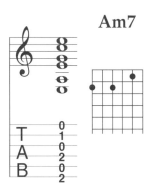
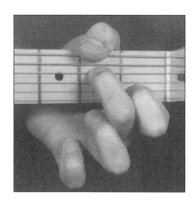

Amaj7

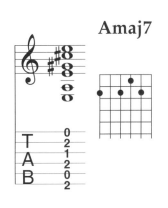
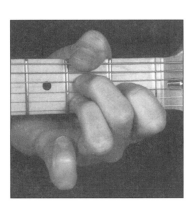

Bm/D

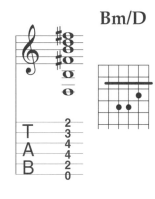
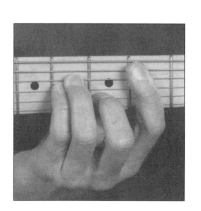

A7

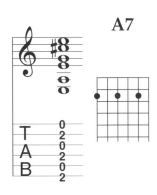

C/E

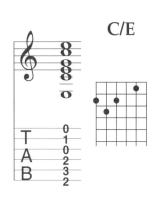

A13

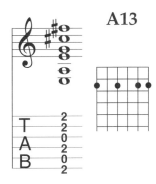
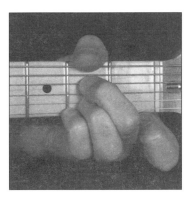

C/D

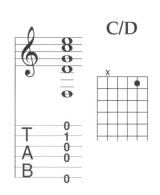
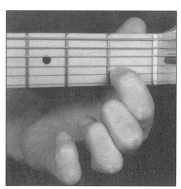

13

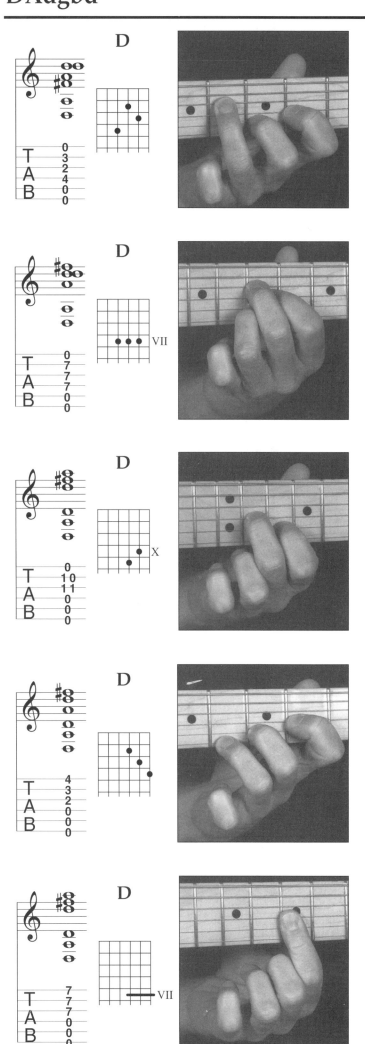

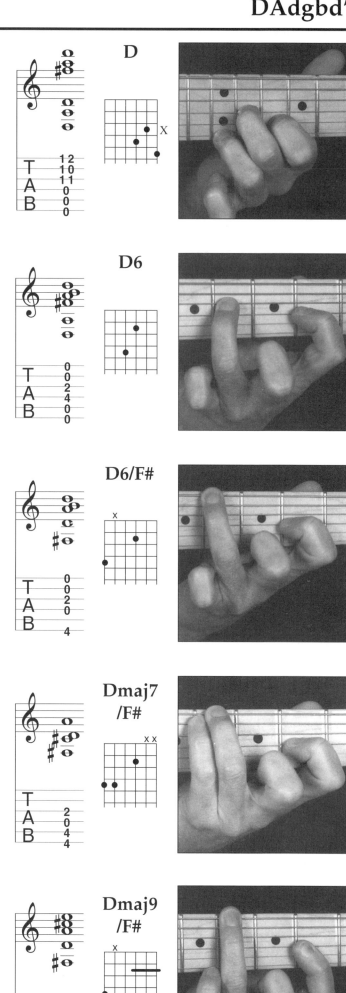

Dmaj7

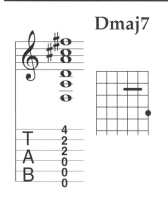
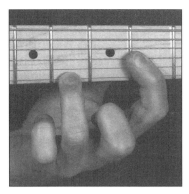

D13

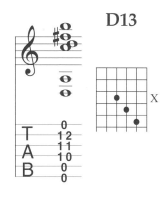
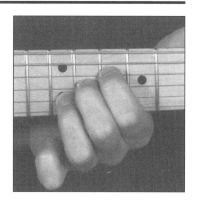

Dadd9

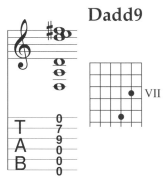

D/C

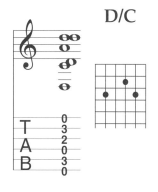
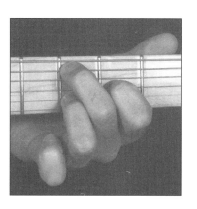

Dmaj9

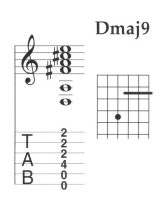
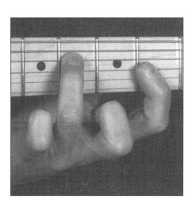

Dm7

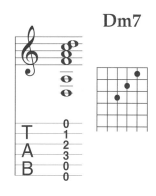

D7

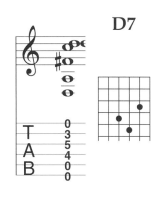
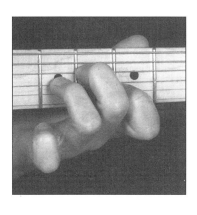

Dm7

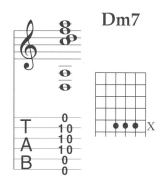

D9

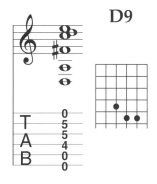
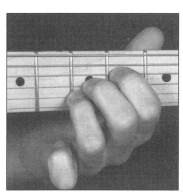

Dm11

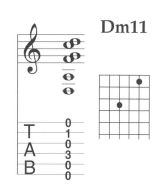
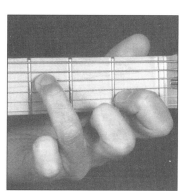

15

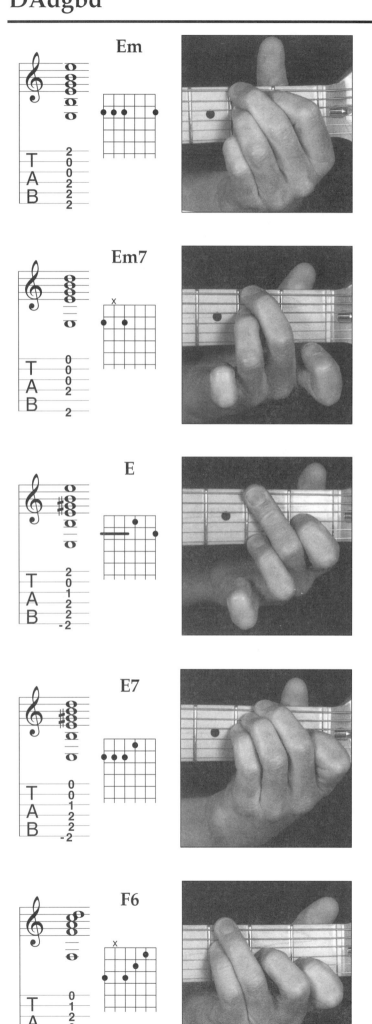

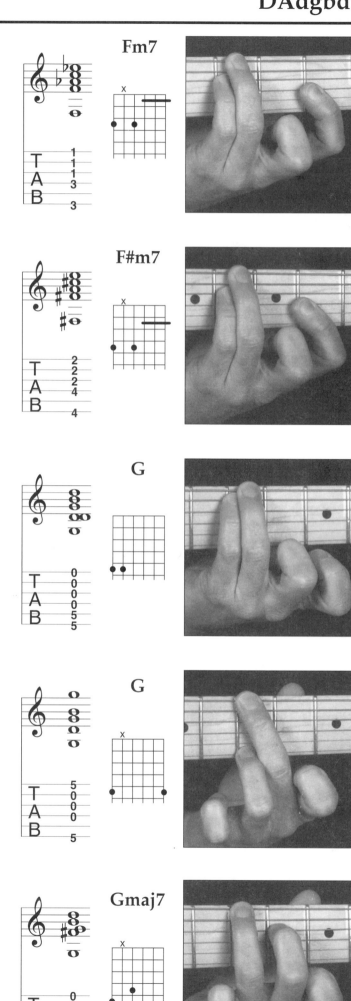

DAdgbd′

DAdgbd′

Gadd9
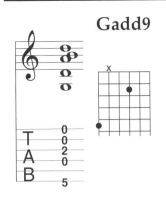 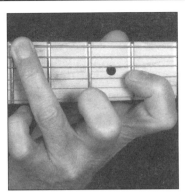 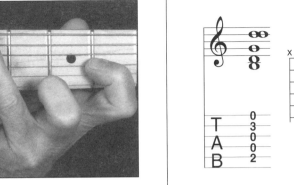

TAB
0
0 2 0
0
5

G/B
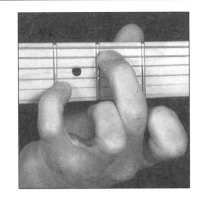

TAB
0
3
0
0
2

G7
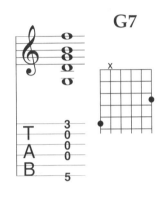 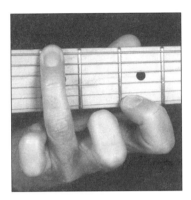

TAB
3 0 0 0
0
5

Aadd9
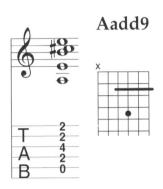 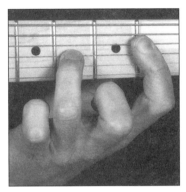

TAB
2 2
4 2
0

Gm
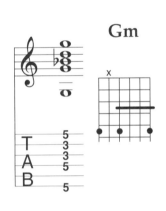 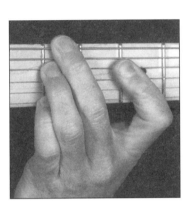

TAB
5
3
3 5
5

Aadd11
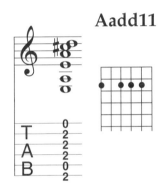 

TAB
0
2
2
2 0 2

Gm7
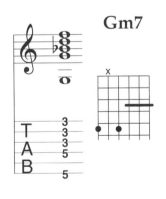 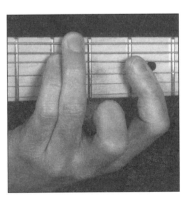

TAB
3 3
3
5
5

Aadd9 add11
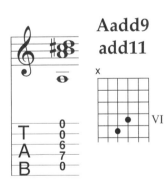 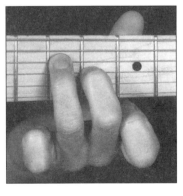

VI

TAB
0
0
6 7
0

Gm/Bb
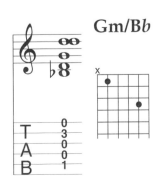 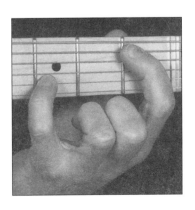

TAB
0
3
0 0
1

Aadd9 add11
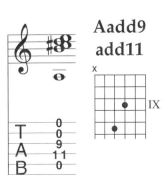 

IX

TAB
0
0 9
9
11
0

17

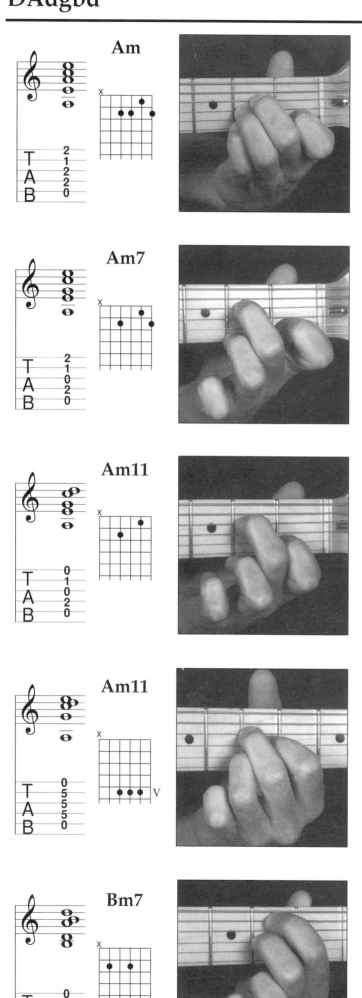
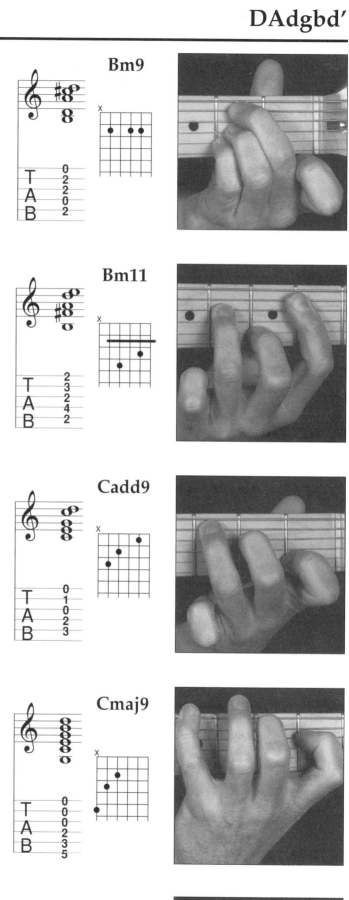

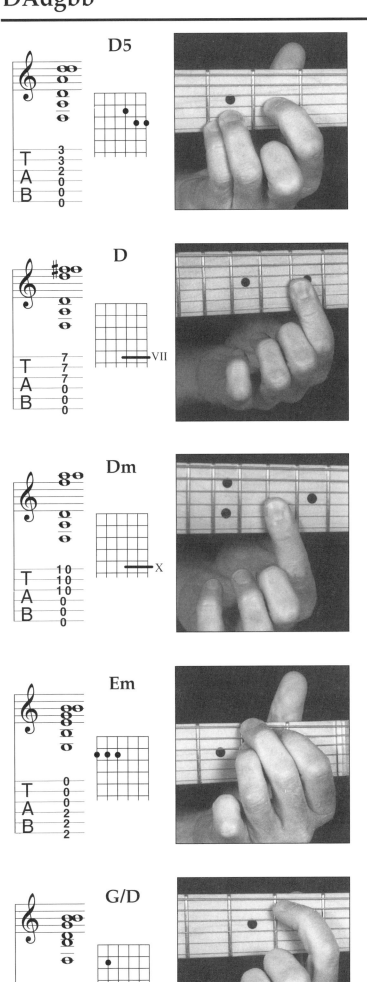

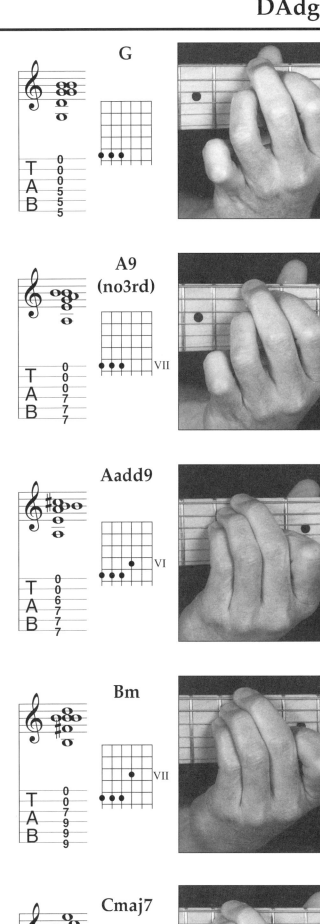

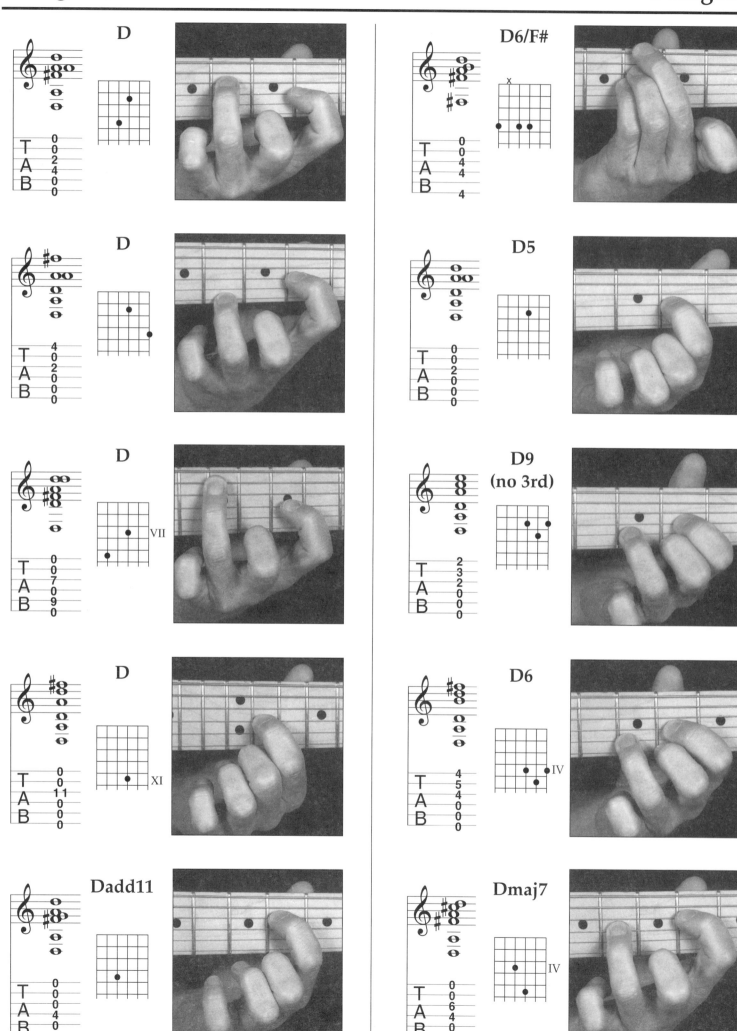

Dmaj7

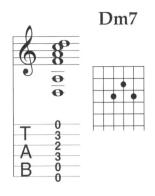

```
    4
    4
    2
    0
T   0
A   0
B
```

Dmaj7

```
    4
    5
    6
T   0
A   0
B   0
```
IV

D7

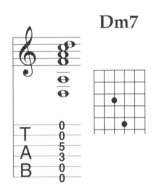

```
    0
    0
    5
T   4
A   0
B
```

Dm

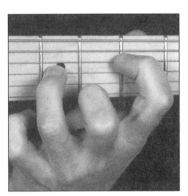

```
    0
    0
    2
T   3
A   0
B   0
```

Dm

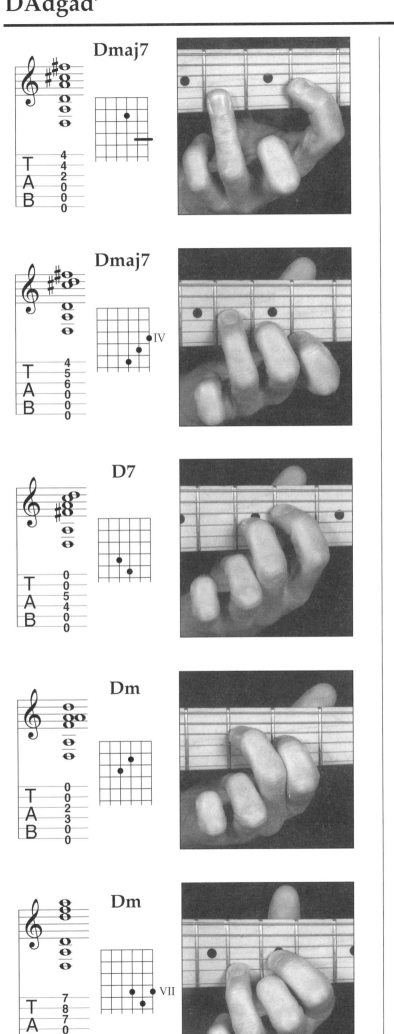

```
    7
    8
    7
T   0
A   0
B   0
```
VII

Dm7

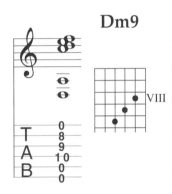

```
    0
    3
    2
T   3
A   0
B   0
```

Dm7

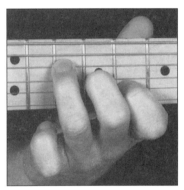

```
    0
    0
    5
T   3
A   0
B   0
```

Dm9

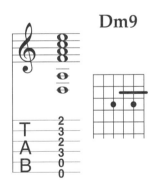

```
    0
    8
    9
T   10
A   0
B   0
```
VIII

Dm9

```
    2
    3
    2
T   3
A   0
B   0
```

Dm13

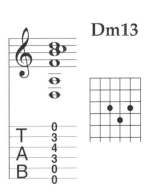

```
    0
    3
    4
T   3
A   0
B   0
```

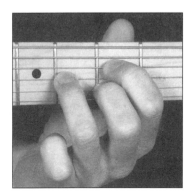

DAdgad'

Dm11

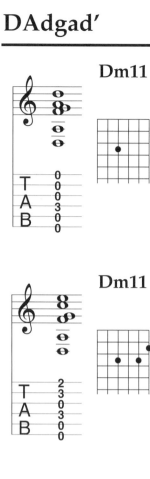

Dm11

Ebmaj7

Em7

Em11

Em11

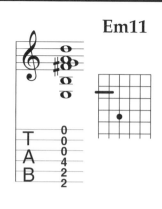

E5

E

E7

E11

F

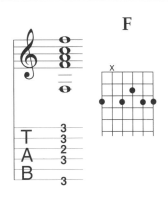

F6

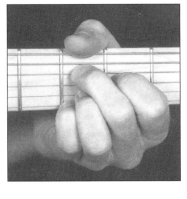

F6 add9

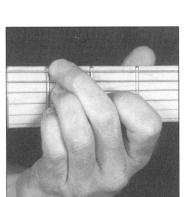

Fmaj9/A

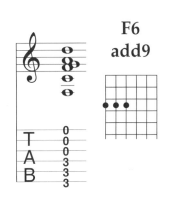

G5

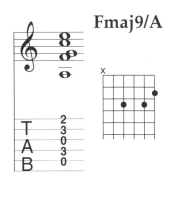

G

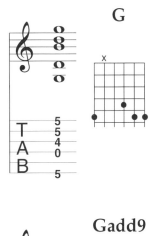
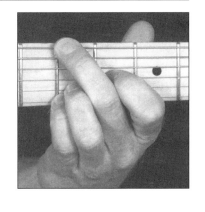

Gadd9

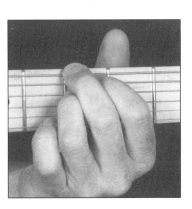

Gmaj9

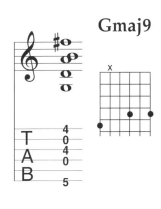

Gadd11

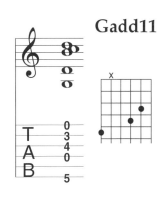

Gmaj9

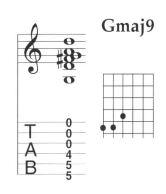

DAdgad'

DAdgad'

G9
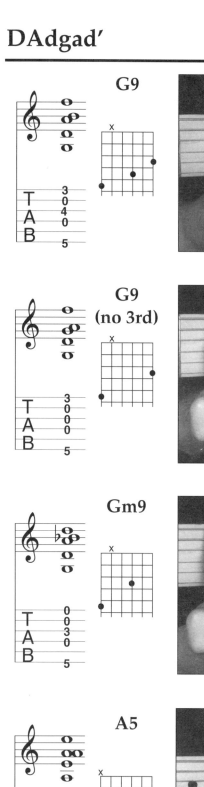

A11
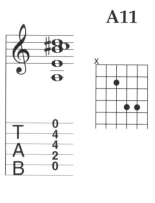
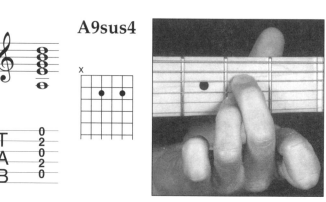

G9 (no 3rd)

A9sus4
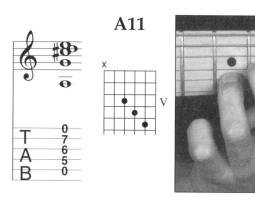

Gm9

A11

A5

A11
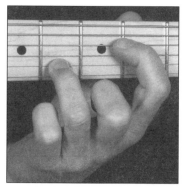

A

A11
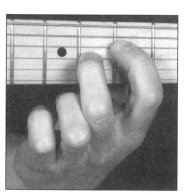

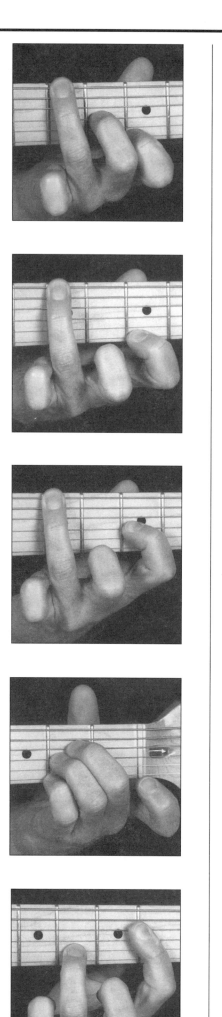
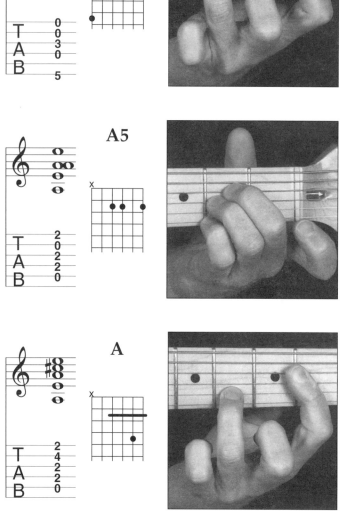
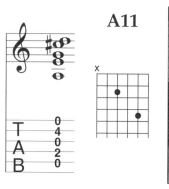
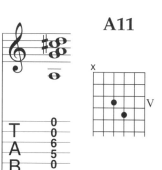

Am

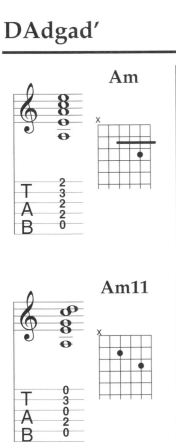

```
T  2
A  3
   2
   2
B  0
```

Am11

```
T  0
A  3
   0
   2
B  0
```

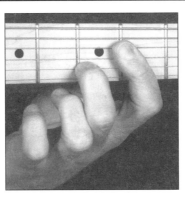

Am11

```
T  0
A  3
   4
   5
B  0
```

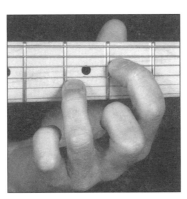

Am11

```
T  0
A  3
   4
   2
B  0
```

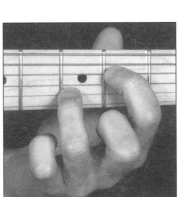

B♭maj7

```
T  0
A  0
   0
   3
   3
B  1
```

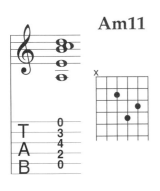
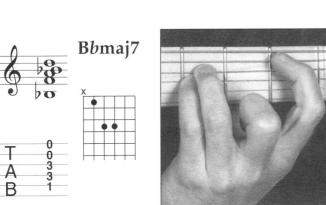

Bm7

```
T  0
A  2
   2
   0
B  2
```

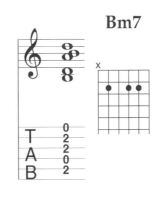

Bm9

```
T  0
A  4
   4
   4
B  2
```

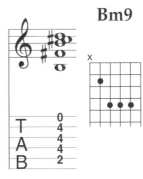
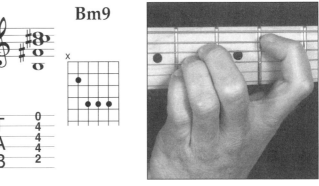

C6 add9

```
T  0
A  0
   0
   2
   3
B  2
```

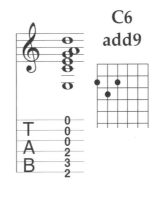

Cadd9

```
T  0
A  3
   0
   2
B  3
```

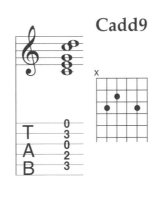
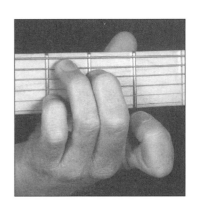

Cm9

```
T  0
A  3
   0
   1
B  3
```

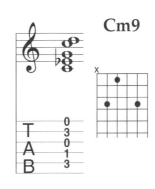
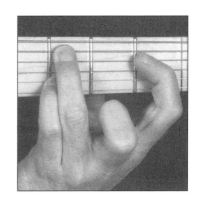

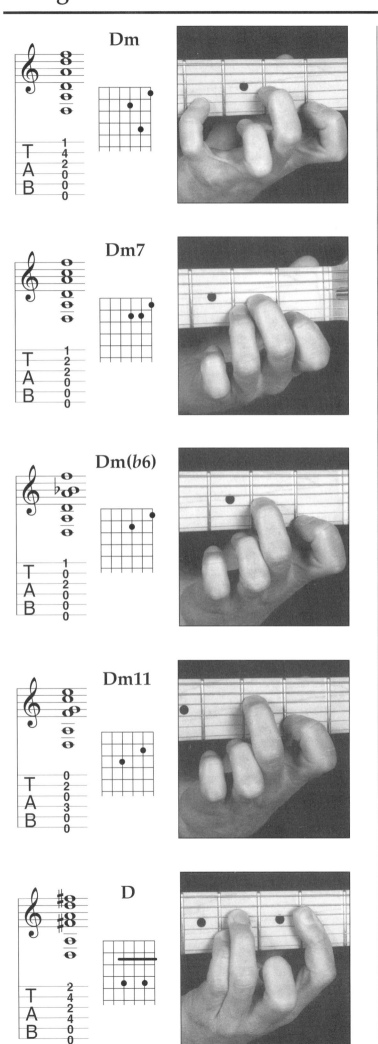

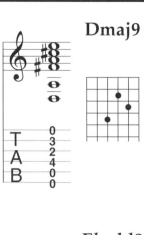
Dmaj9
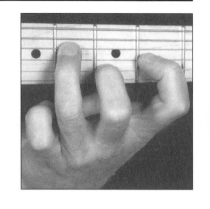

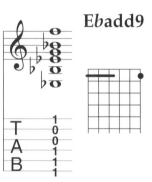
Ebadd9

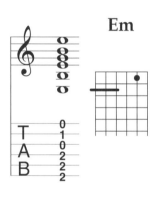
Em
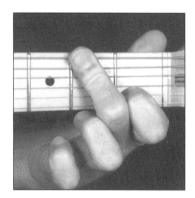

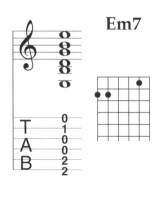
Em7
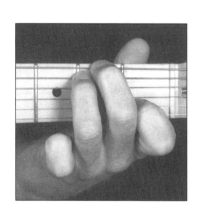

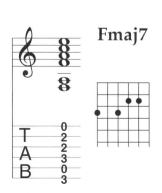
Fmaj7

26

Gm

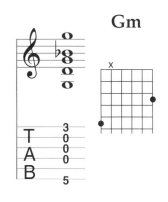
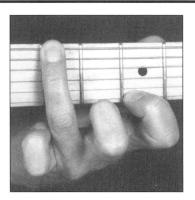

A7

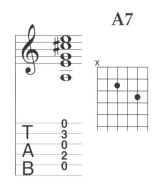
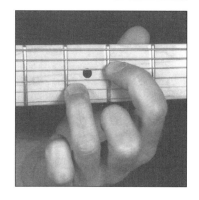

Gm6

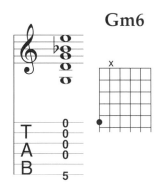
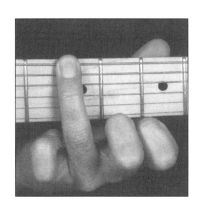

A7(b9)

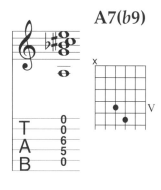

Gm11

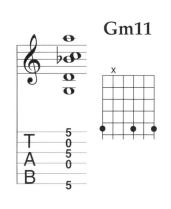
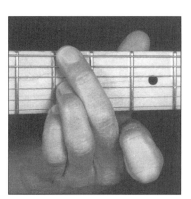

B♭maj7

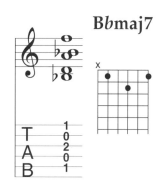
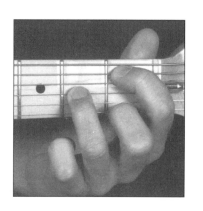

Am7

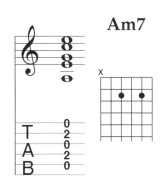
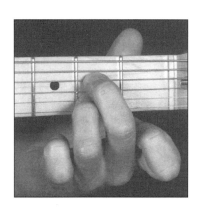

C

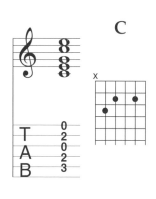

Am11

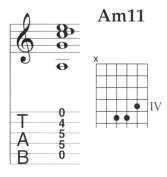
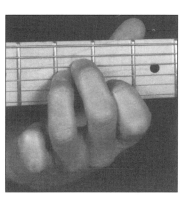

C7

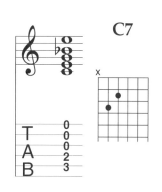
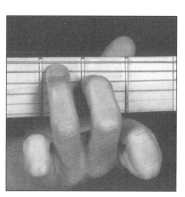

D

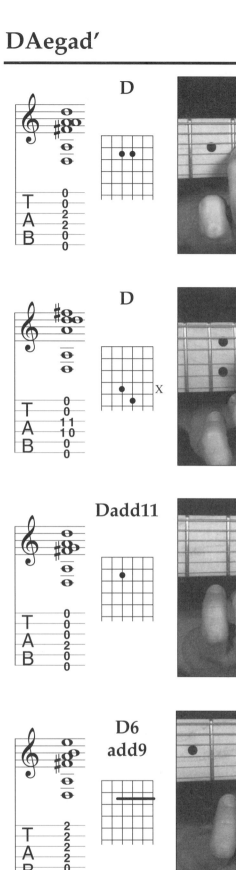

D

Dadd11

D6 add9

D7sus4

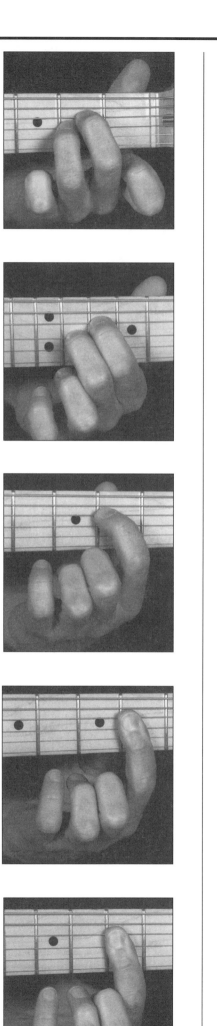

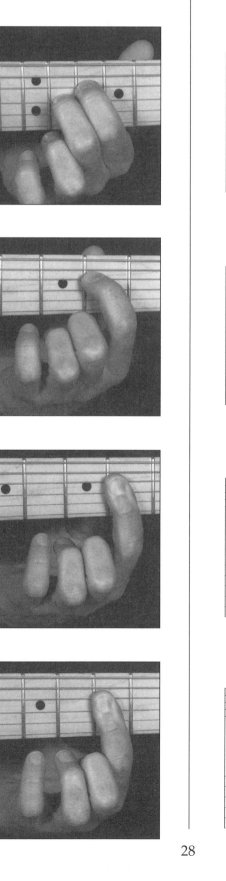

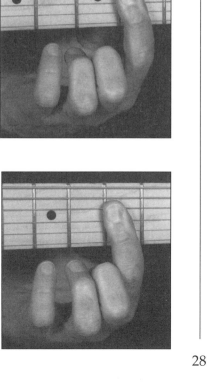

Dm

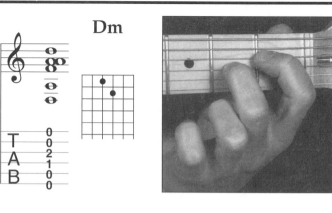

Dm7

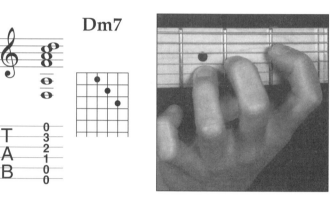

Dm11

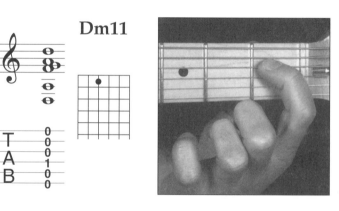

Em11

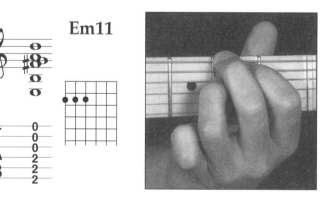

F6/9

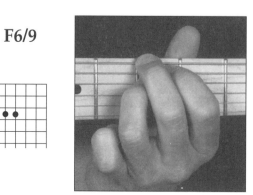

DAegad'

F#m9(b6)

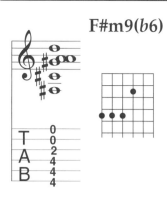
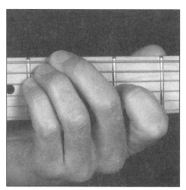
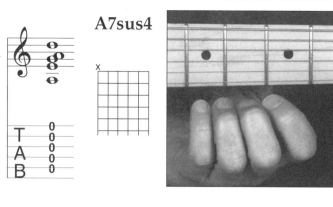

A7sus4

Gadd9

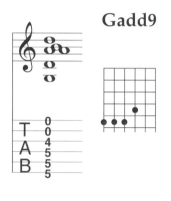
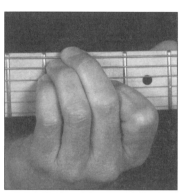
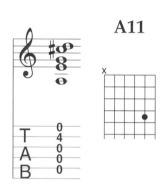
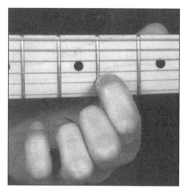

A11

G6 add9

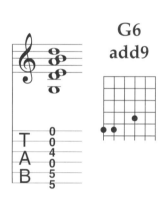
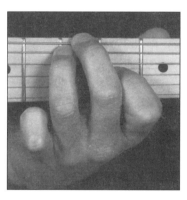
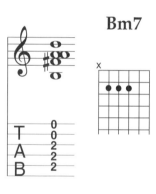

Bm7

Gm9

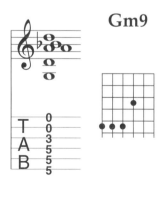
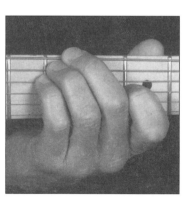
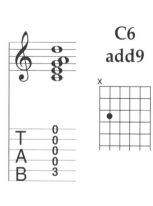
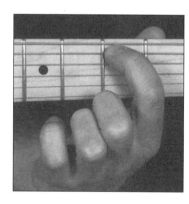

C6 add9

A

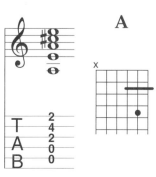
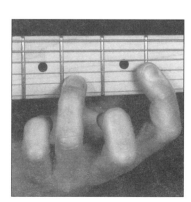
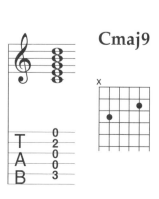
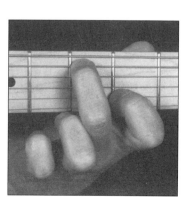

Cmaj9

29

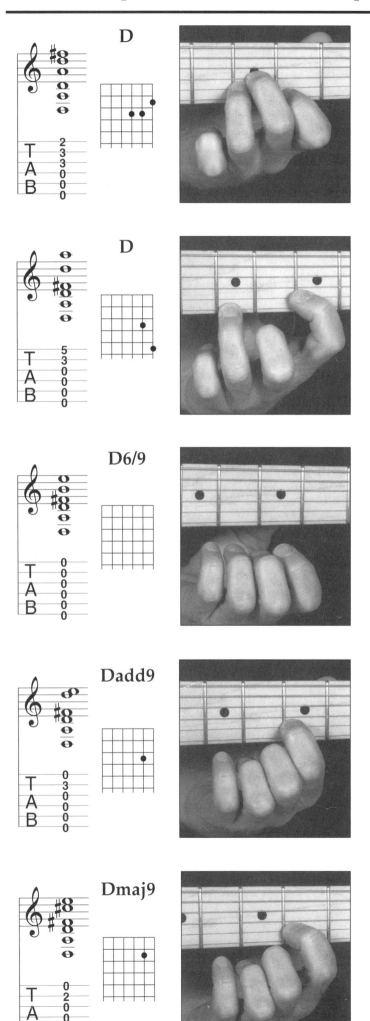

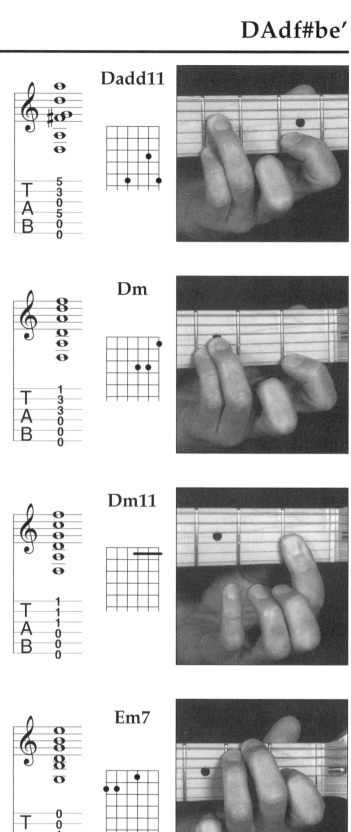

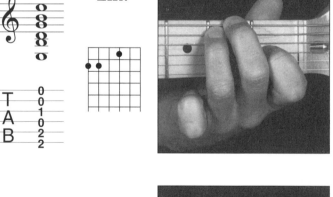

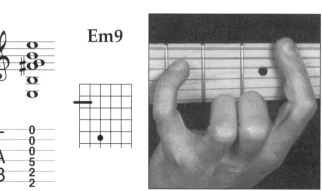

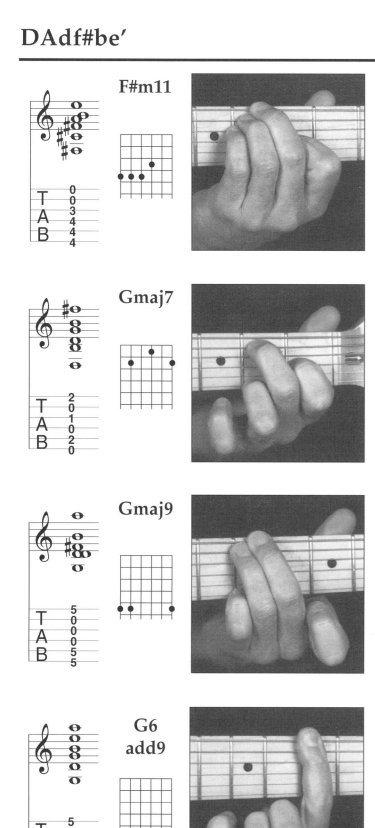
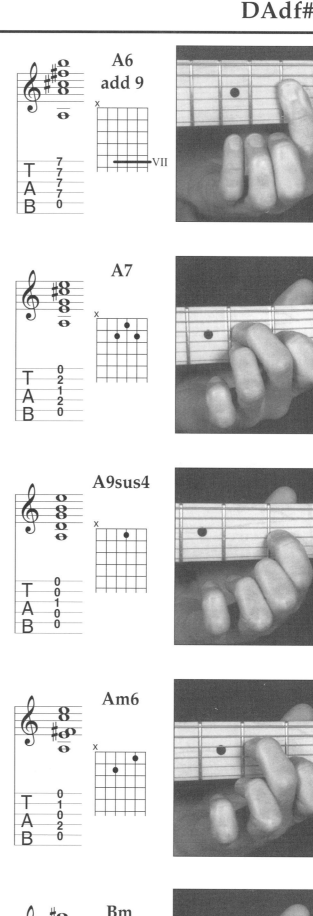

F#m11

```
T  0
A  3
   4
B  4
   4
```

Gmaj7

```
T  2
   0  1  0
A  1  0
   0  2
B  0
```

Gmaj9

```
   5
T  0  0  0
   0  0
A  0
   5
B  5
```

G6
add9

```
   5
T  5
   5
A  5
   5
B  5
```

Gm6

```
T  0
   3
A  4
   0
B  5
   5
```

A6
add 9

x

```
T  7
   7
   7
A  7
   0
B
```
VII

A7

x

```
T  0
   2
   1
A  2
   0
B
```

A9sus4

x

```
T  0
   0
   1
A  0
   0
B
```

Am6

x

```
T  0
   1
   0
A  2
   0
B
```

Bm

x

```
T  2
   0
   0
A  0
   0
B  2
```

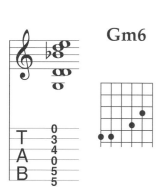
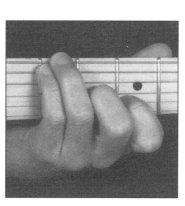
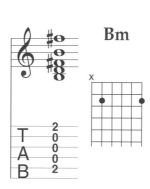
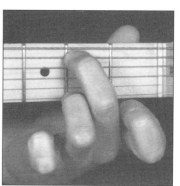

D

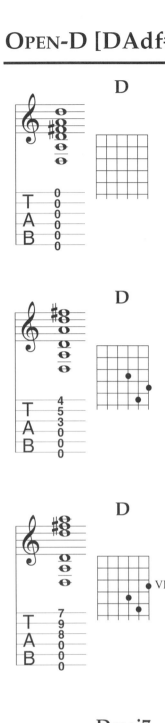

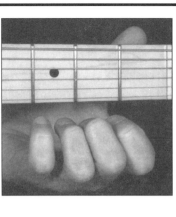

D

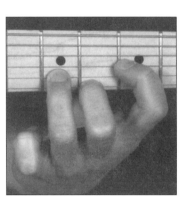

D

Dmaj7

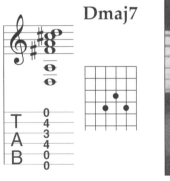

Dmaj7

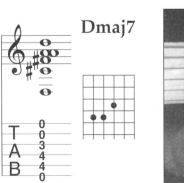

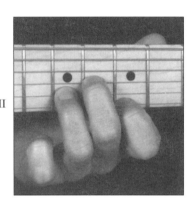

Dmaj7

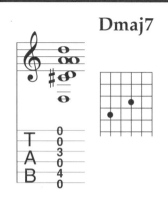

Dadd9

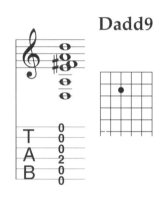

D7

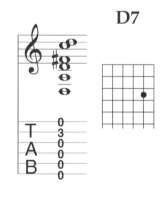

D7 (no 3rd)

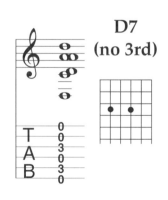

D9

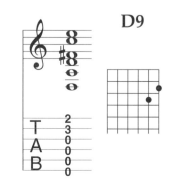

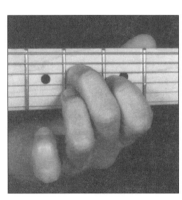

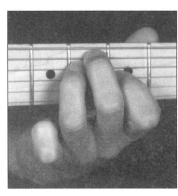

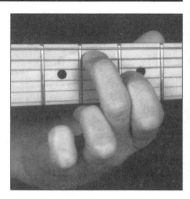

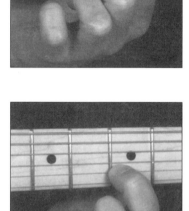

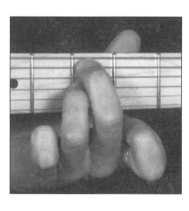

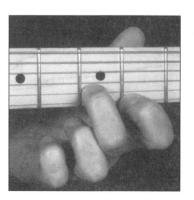

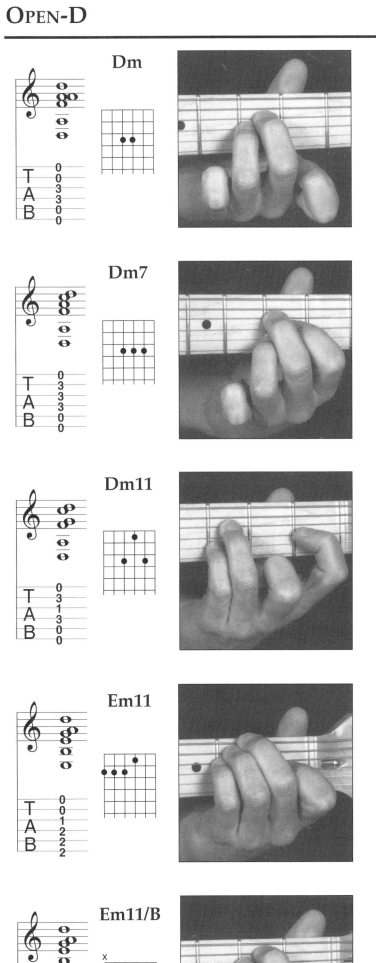

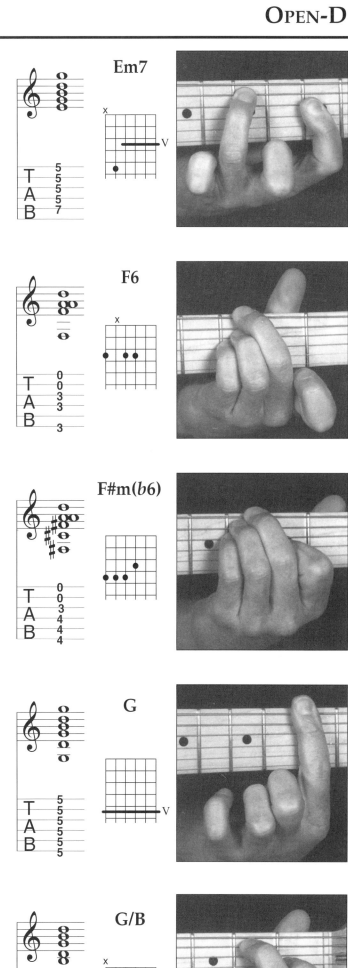

Gadd9/B

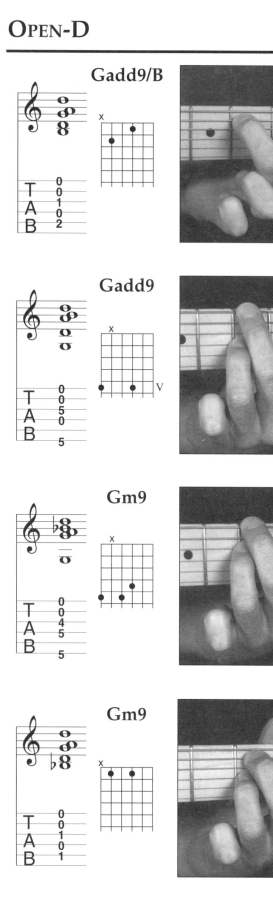

Gadd9

Gm9

Gm9

A

Aadd9

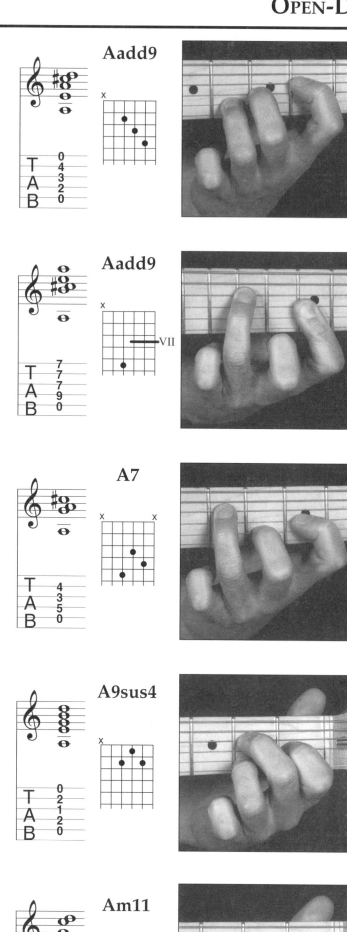

Aadd9

A7

A9sus4

Am11

Am11

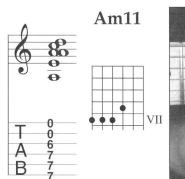
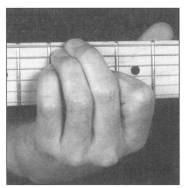

VII

```
T 0
A 0
  6
B 7
  7
  7
```

D

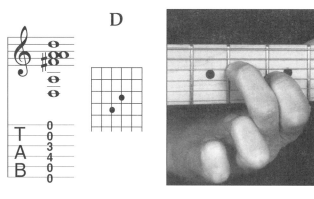

```
T 0
A 0
  3
B 4
  0
  0
```

Bm

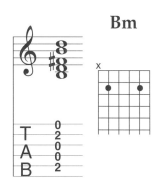

x

```
T 0
A 2
  0
B 0
  2
```

Gadd9/A

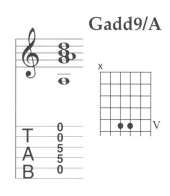
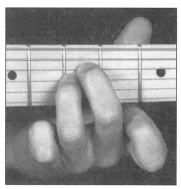

x

V

```
T 0
A 0
  5
B 5
  0
```

Cadd9

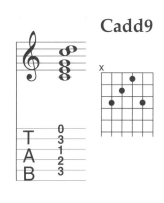

x

```
T 0
A 3
  1
B 2
  3
```

Aadd11

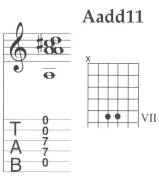
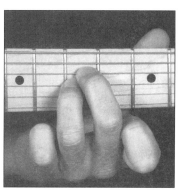

x

VII

```
T 0
A 0
  7
B 0
```

C6add9 /E

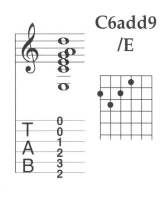
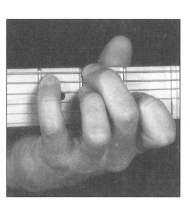

```
T 0
A 0
  1
B 2
  3
  2
```

D6 (no3rd)

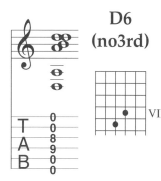
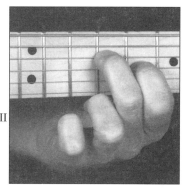

VIII

```
T 0
A 0
  8
B 9
  0
  0
```

Dadd9 sus4

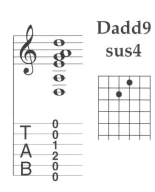
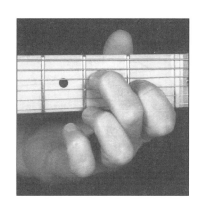

```
T 0
A 0
  1
B 2
  0
  0
```

Aadd11

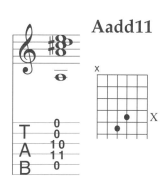
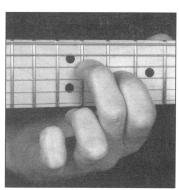

x

X

```
T 0
A 0
  10
B 11
  0
```

35

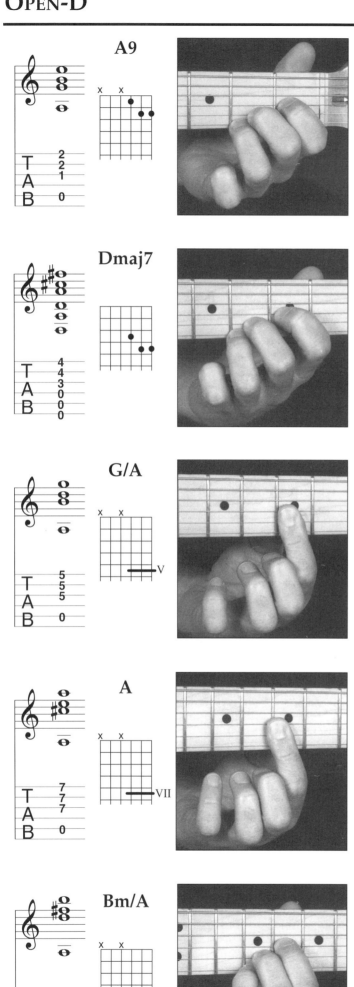

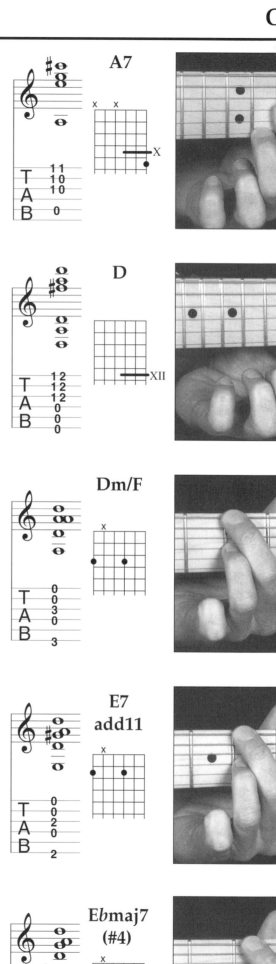

OPEN D-MINOR [DAdfad']

OPEN D-MINOR

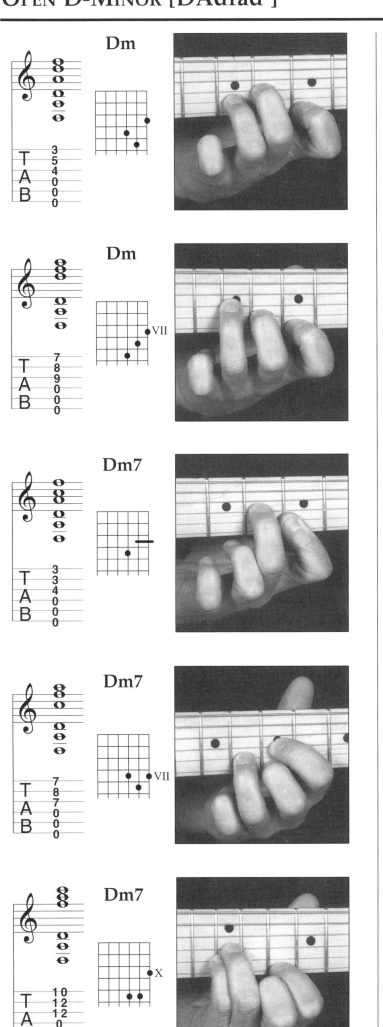

Dm

Dm

Dm7

Dm7

Dm7

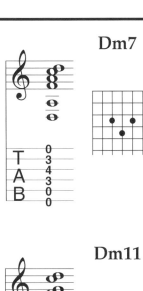

Dm7

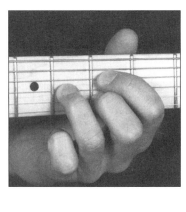

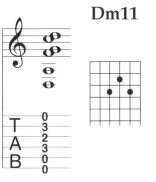

Dm11

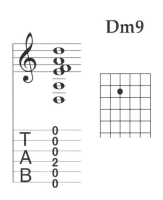

Dm9

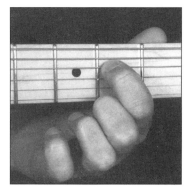

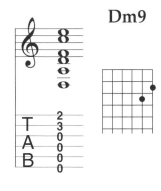

Dm9

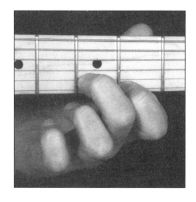

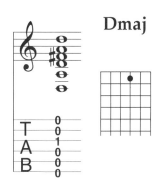

Dmaj

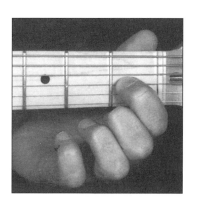

OPEN-D MINOR OPEN-D MINOR

D9

T   0
A   3
B   1
    2
    0
    0
```

## Gm9

```
T   0
A   0
B   2
    0
    1
```

Em

```
T   2
A   2
B   2
    2
    2
    2
```

Gadd9

```
T   0
A   0
B   0
    2
    0
    2
    2
```

F

```
T   3
A   3
B   4
    3
    3
    3
```

Am

```
T   2
A   3
B   4
    2
    0
```

F6

```
T   0
A   0
B   0
    3
    3
    3
```

Am11

```
T   0
A   3
B   2
    2
    0
```

Gm

```
T   5
A   5
B   5
    5
    5
    5
```

Am11

```
T   0
A   7
B   7
    7
    0
```

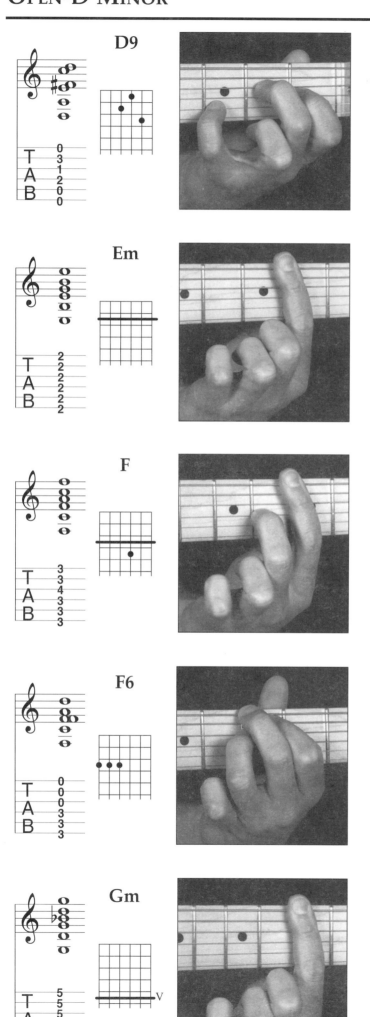
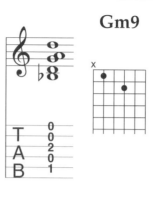
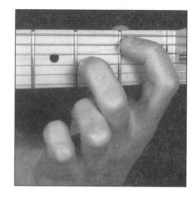
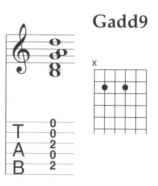
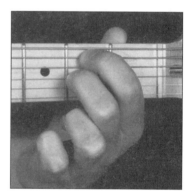
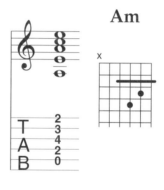
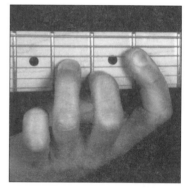
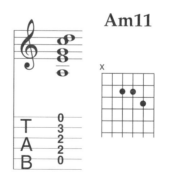
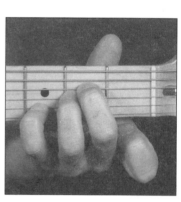
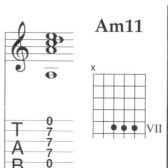
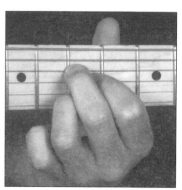

V

VII

38
```

A
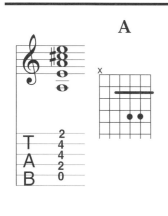

A7add11
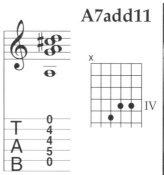
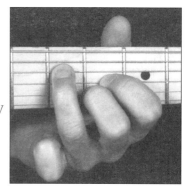

Aadd9
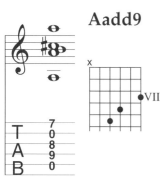
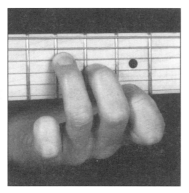

Bb
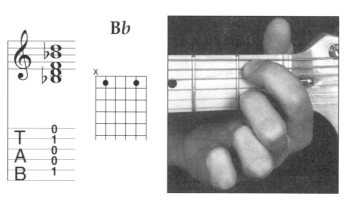

A7
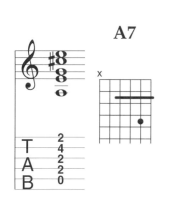
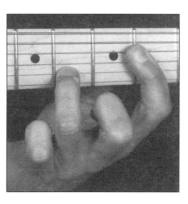

Bbmaj7
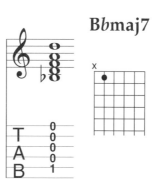
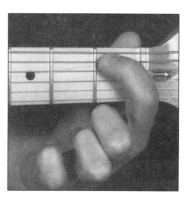

A9sus4
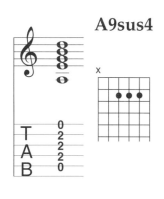

Bbadd9
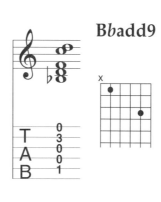
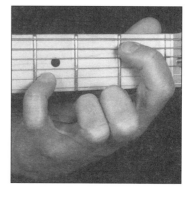

A7sus4
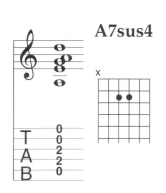
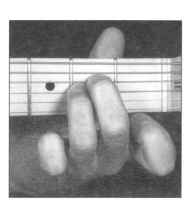

Cadd9
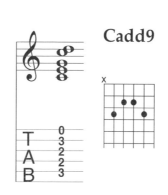
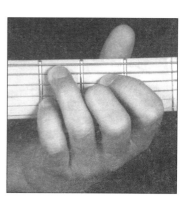

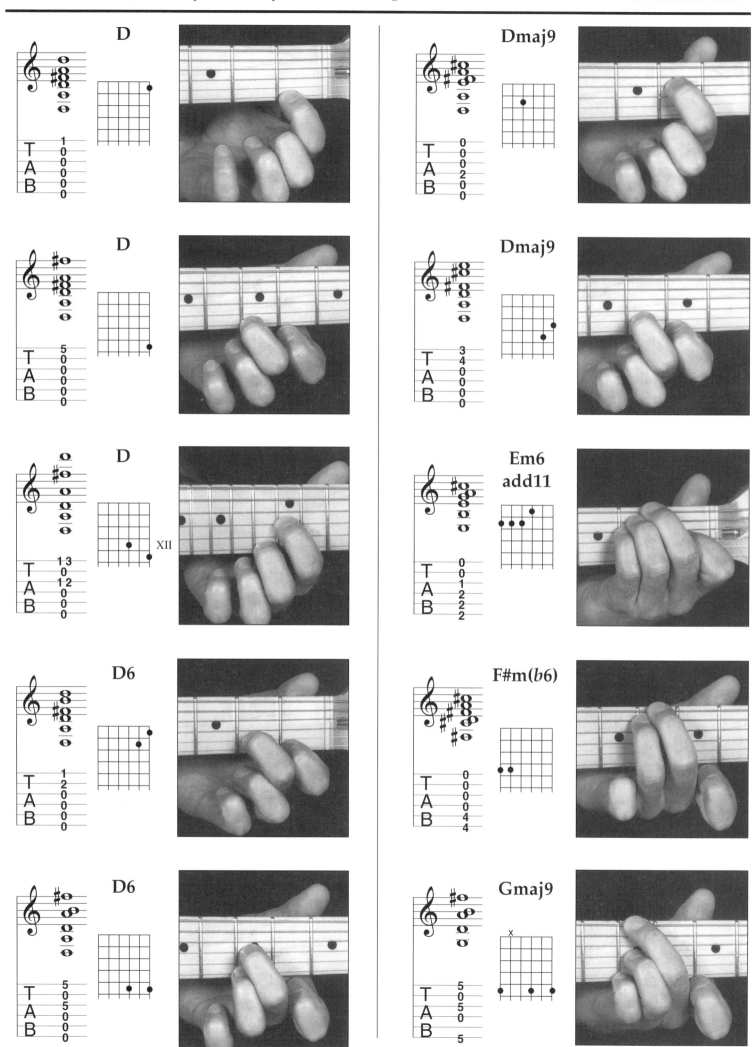

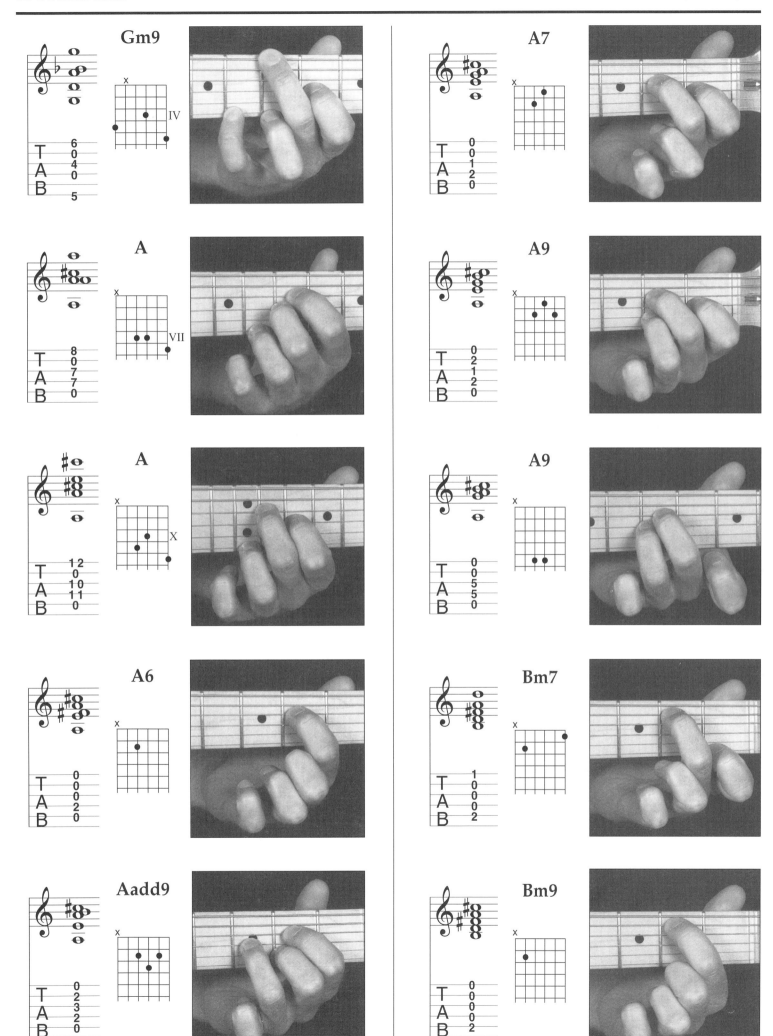

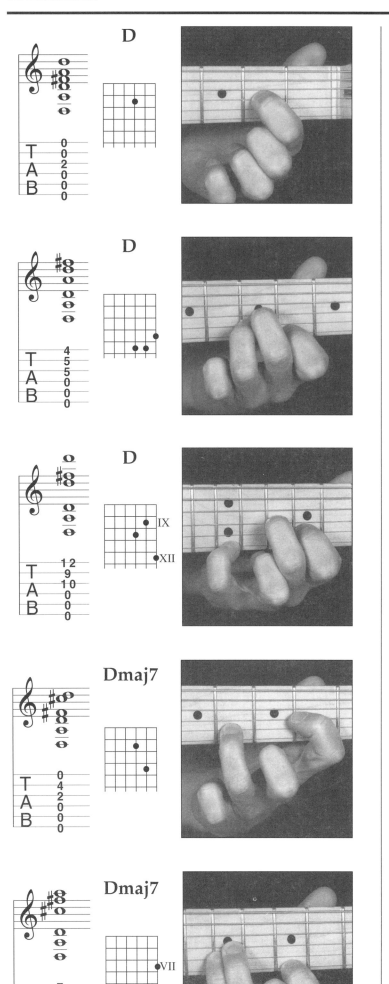

D

Dmaj7
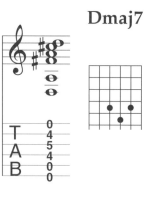
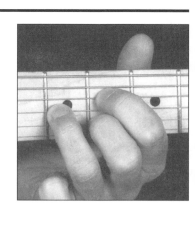

Dadd9
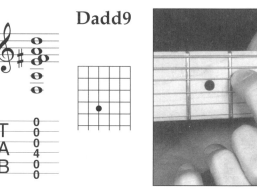

Dadd9
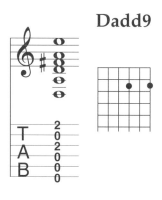
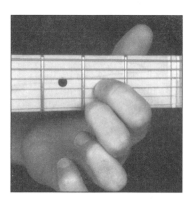

D7
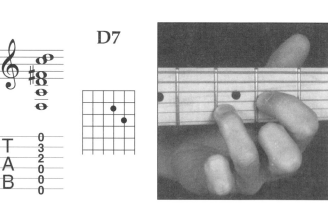

Dmaj7

D9
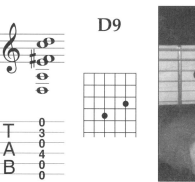
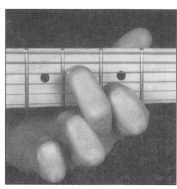

Dm

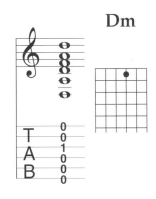
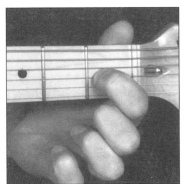

Em

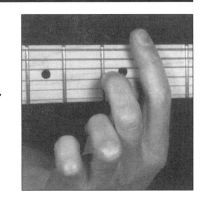

Dm7

Em11

Dm7

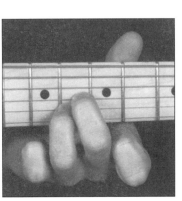

E11

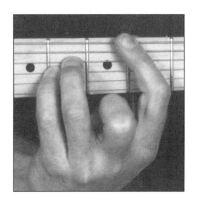

Dm9

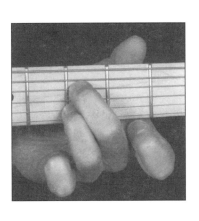

F6 add9

Dm9

Fadd9

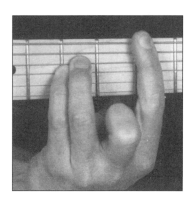

43

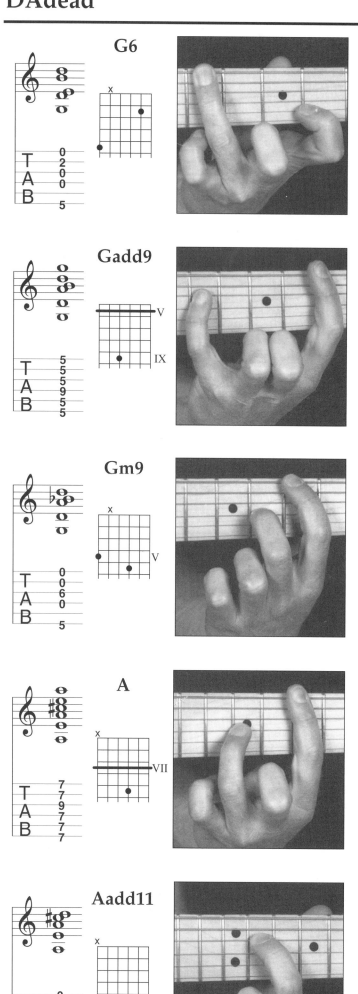

G6

Gadd9

Gm9

A

Aadd11

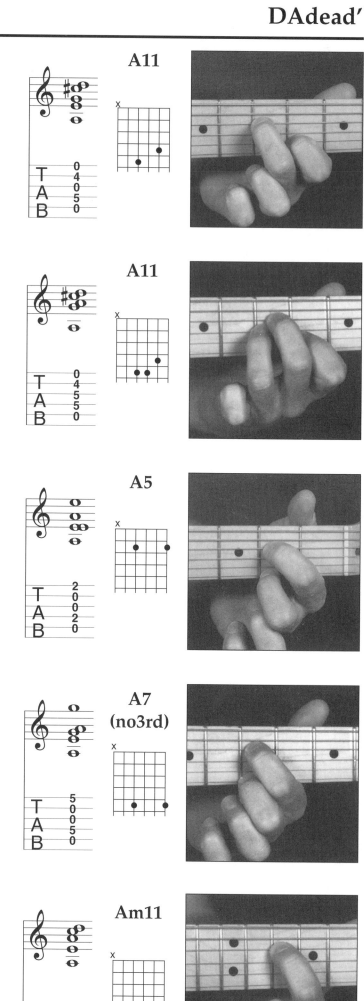

A11

A11

A5

A7
(no3rd)

Am11

Am11

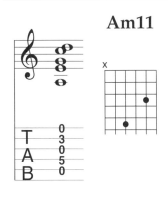

Bbmaj7

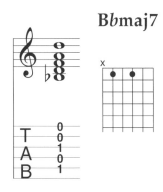

Bm7

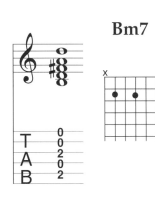

Gadd9

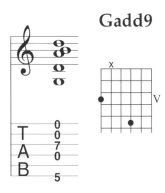
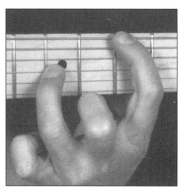

C6add9

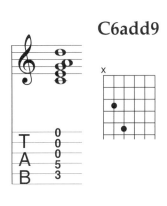
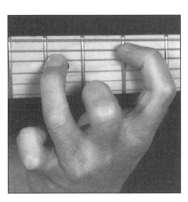

Dm/F

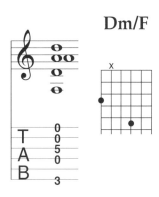
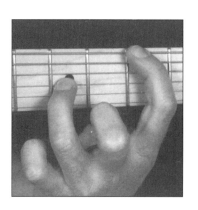

Cadd9

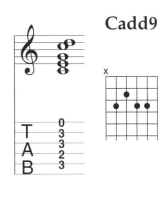

E11

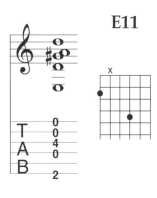
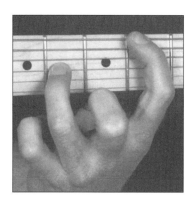

Bb

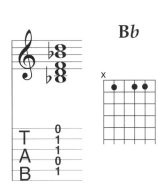

Ebmaj7 (#4)

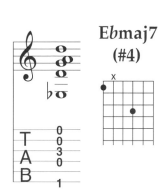
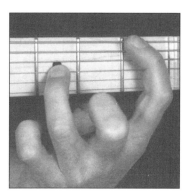

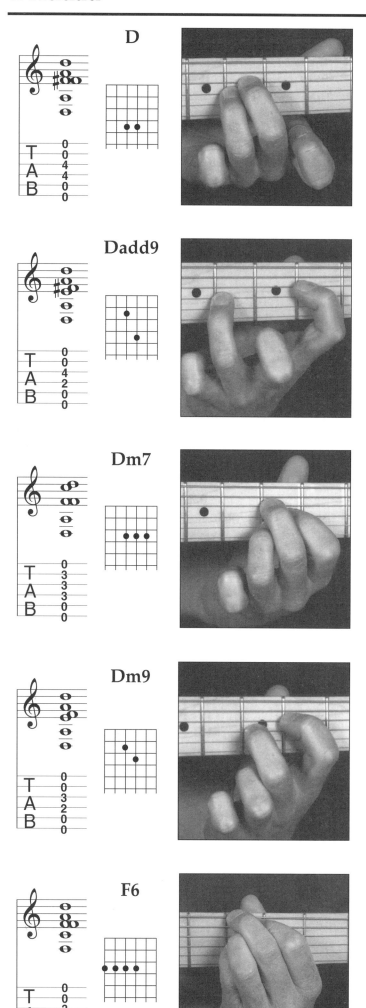

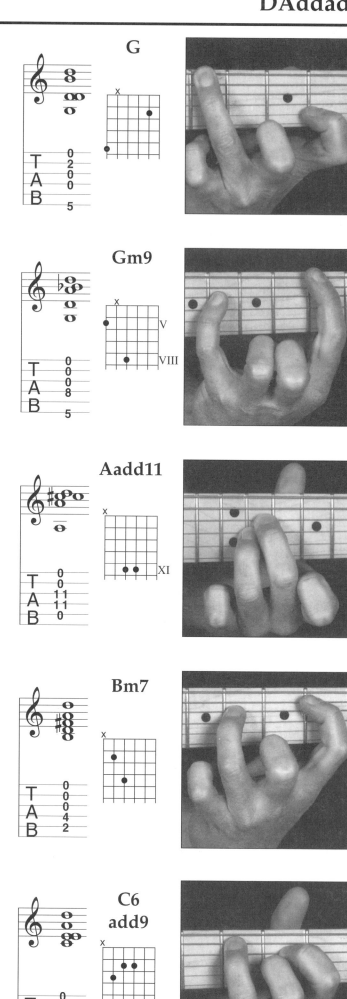

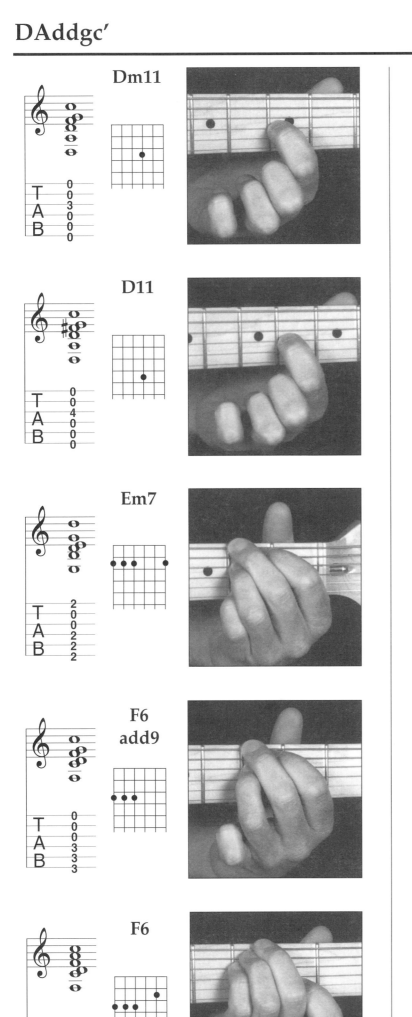

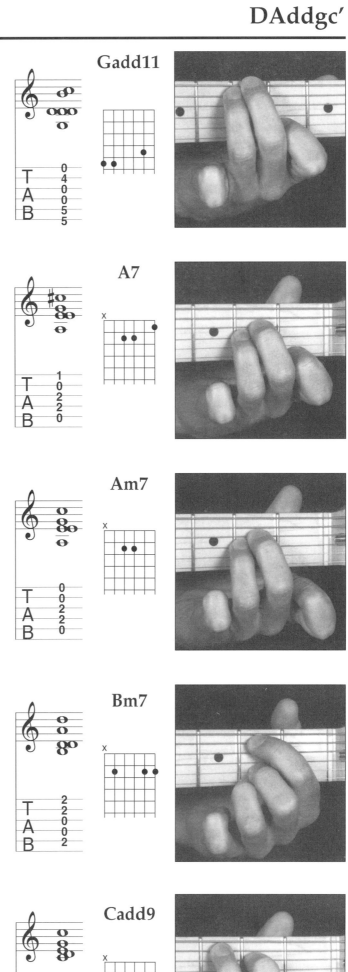

Dm11

D11

Em7

F6 add9

F6

Gadd11

A7

Am7

Bm7

Cadd9

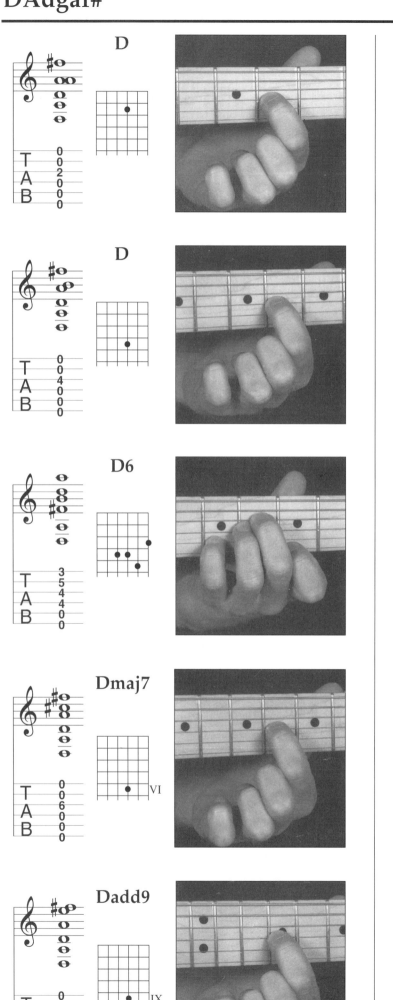

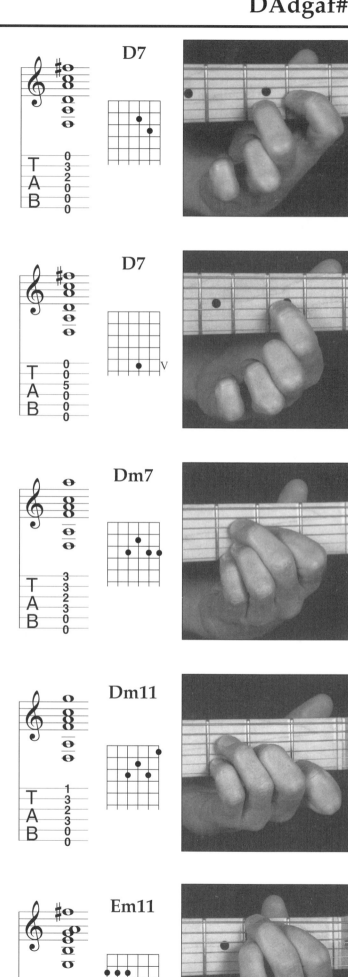

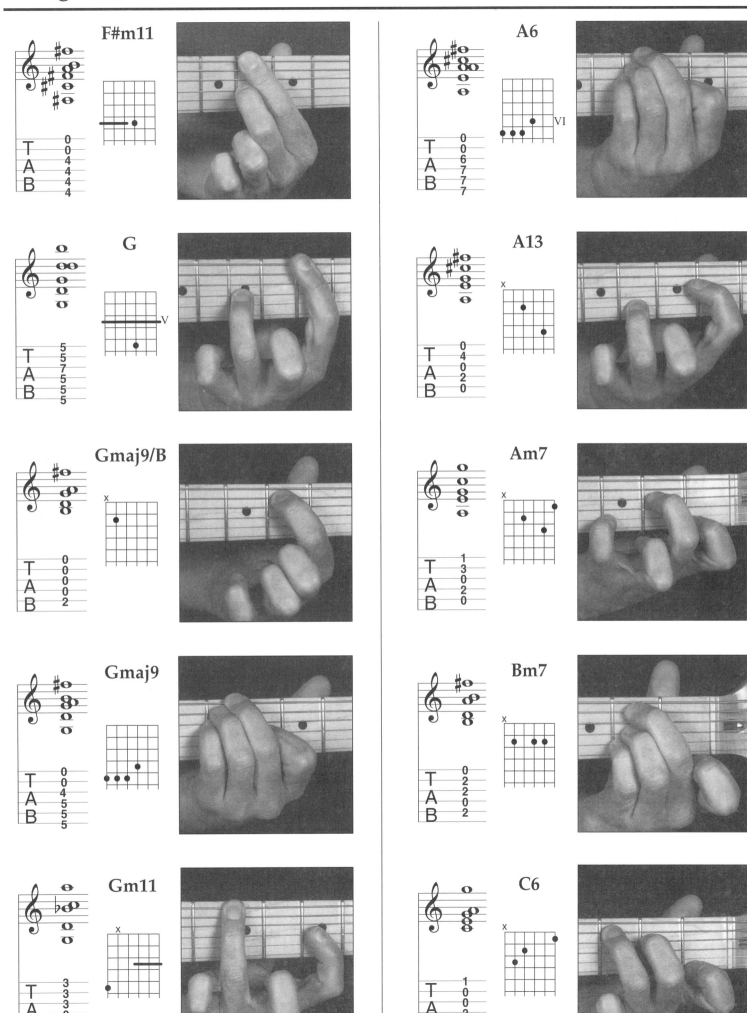

F#m11

G

Gmaj9/B

Gmaj9

Gm11

A6

A13

Am7

Bm7

C6

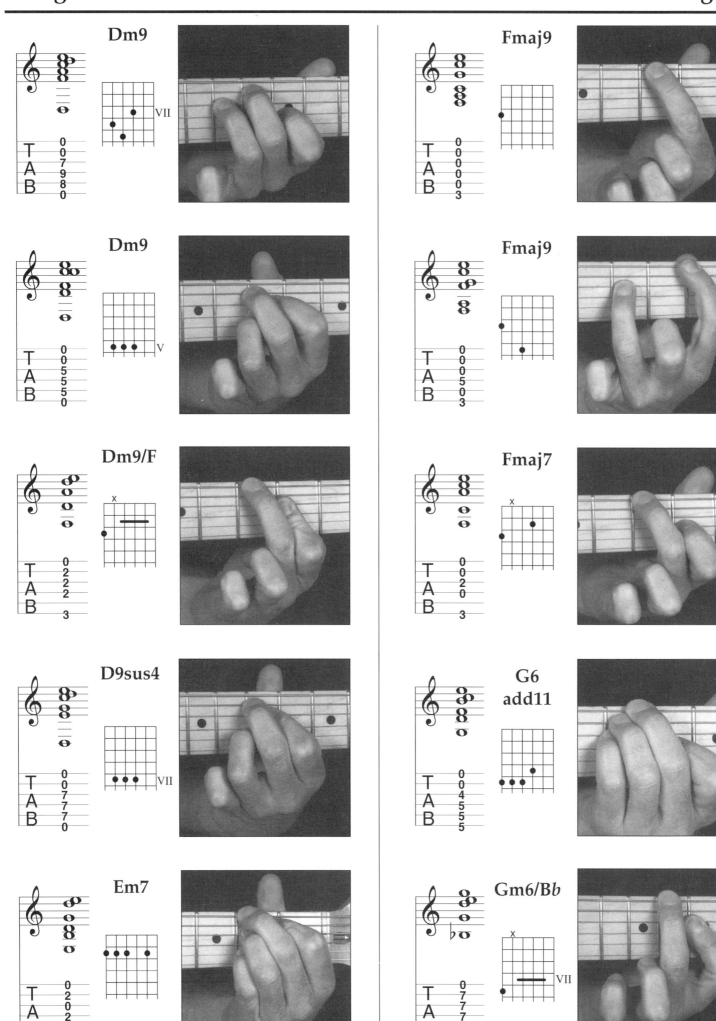

Dm9

Dm9

Dm9/F

D9sus4

Em7

Fmaj9

Fmaj9

Fmaj7

G6 add11

Gm6/B♭

Am7

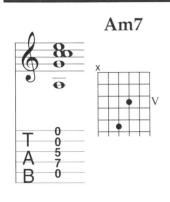

C

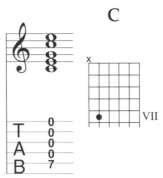
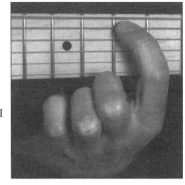

Am7

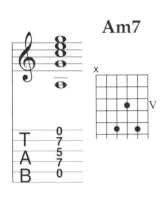
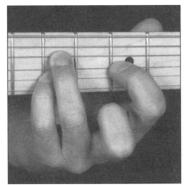

Cadd2

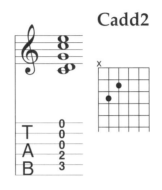
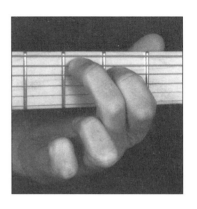

Am7

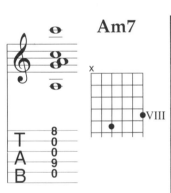
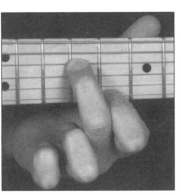

C/Bb

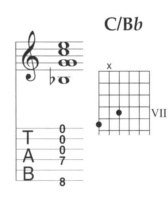
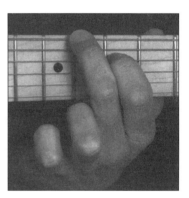

Am11/D

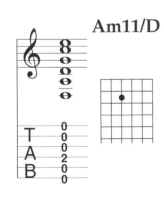
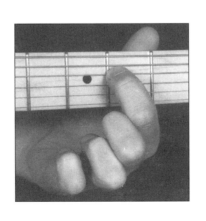

C9/Bb

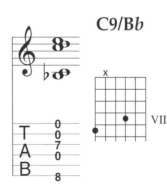
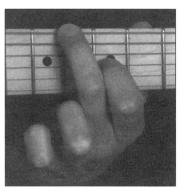

C

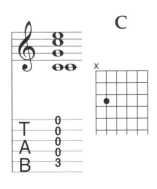
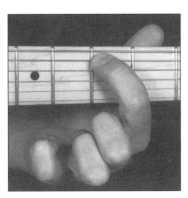

C9/Bb

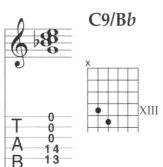

Dadd9
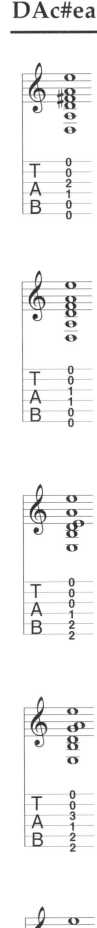
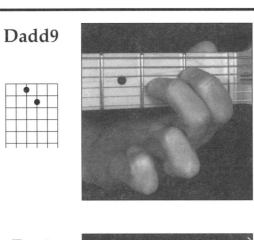

Dm9
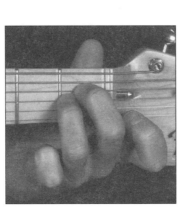

E7sus4
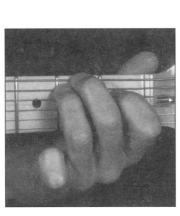

Em11
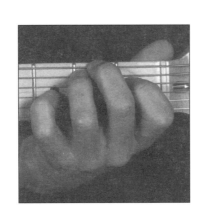

F#m7
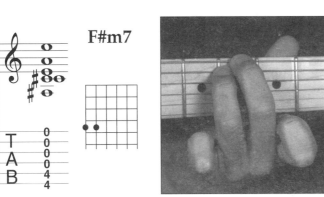

A
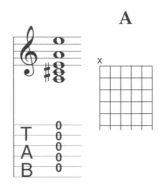
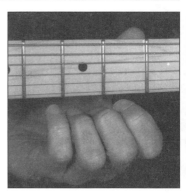

Amaj9
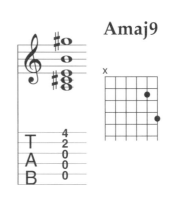
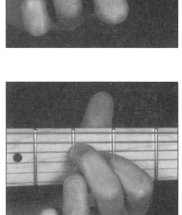

Am7
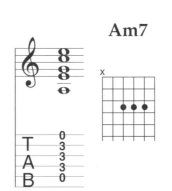

Bm11
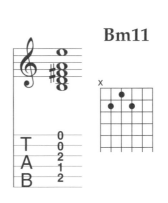
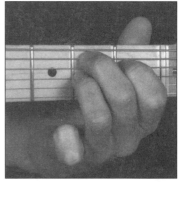

C#m7
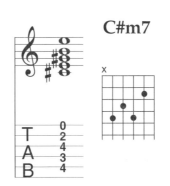
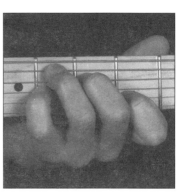

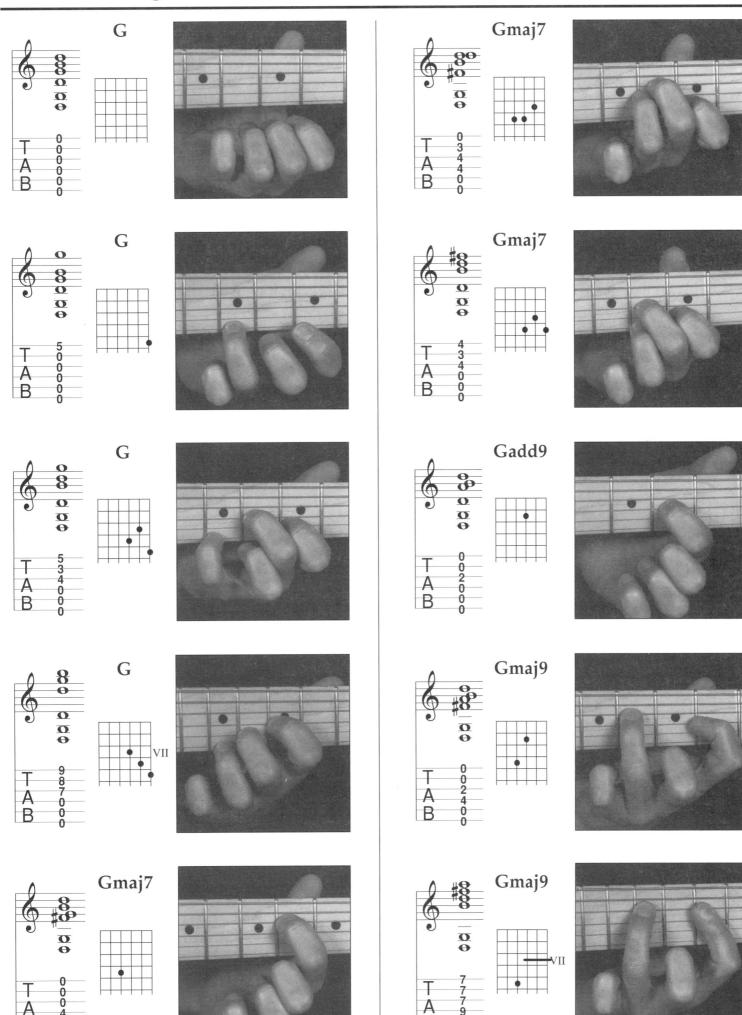

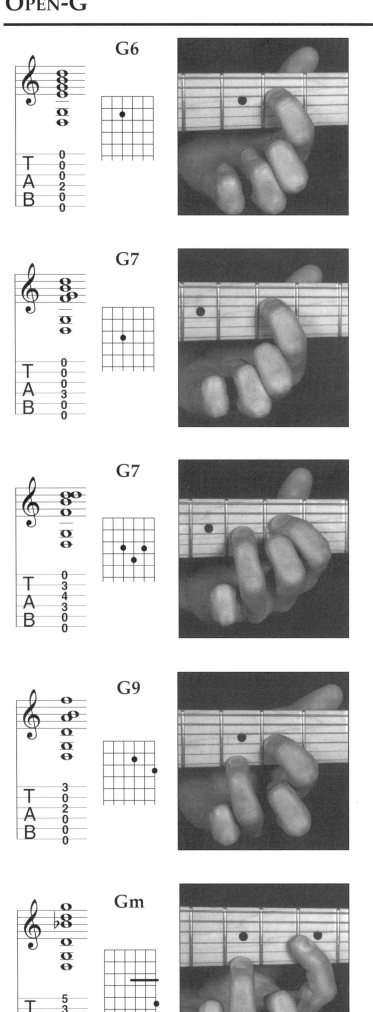
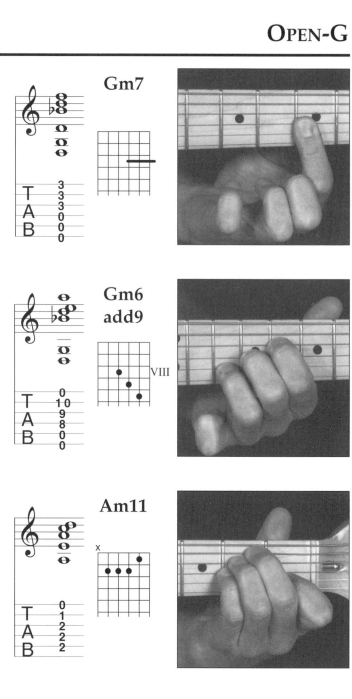
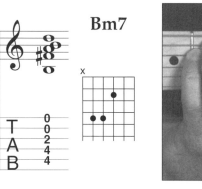
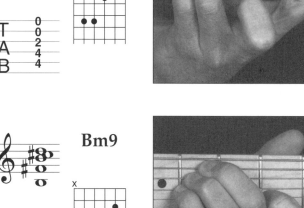

C

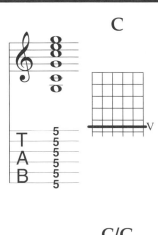
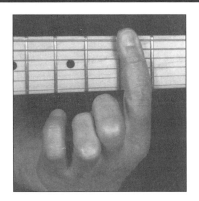

C9/G

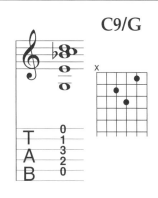

C/G

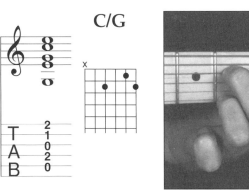

Cm9/G

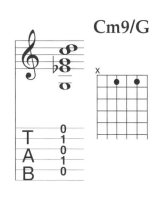

Cadd9/G

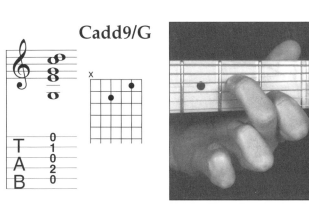

D

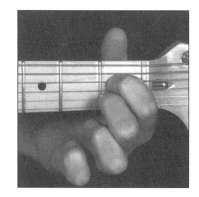

Cadd9/G

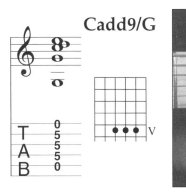

D

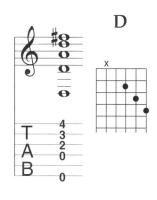
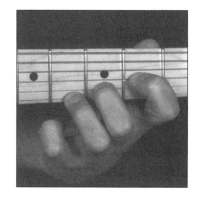

Cadd9/G

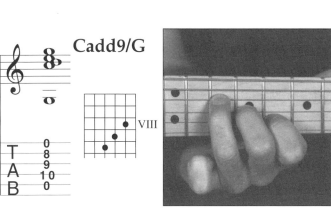

Dadd9

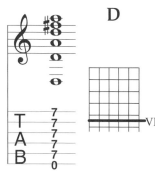
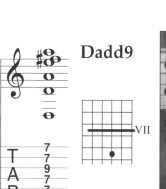
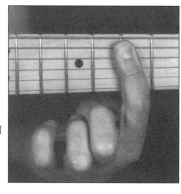
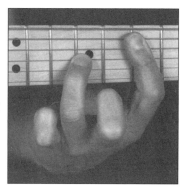

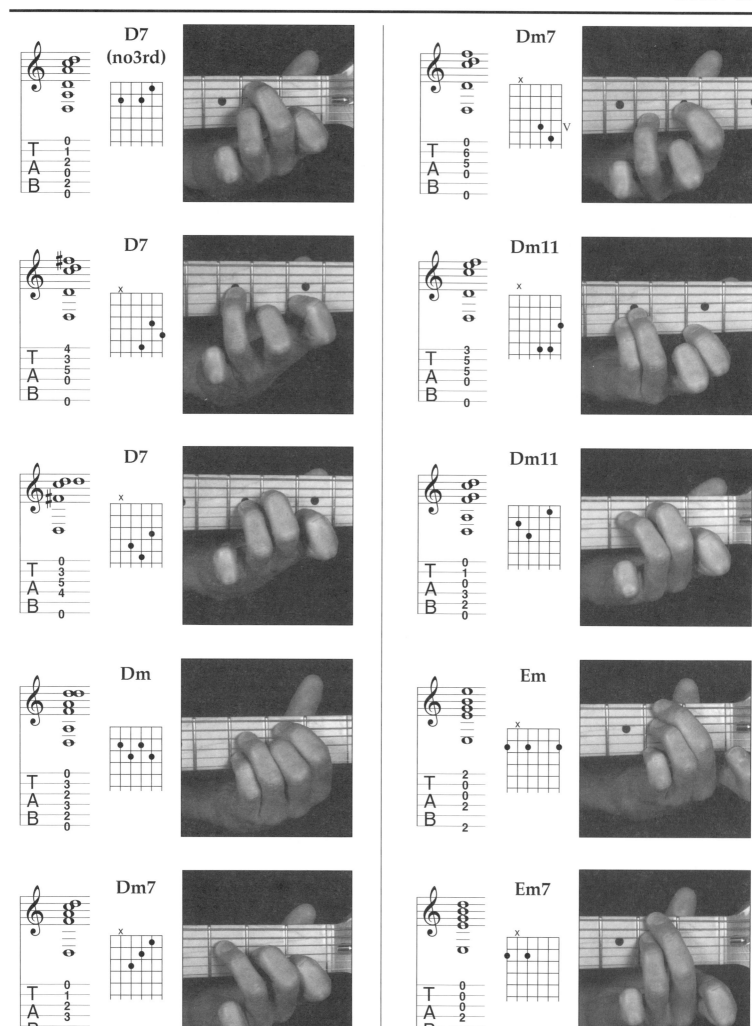

D7
(no3rd)

D7

D7

Dm

Dm7

Dm7

Dm11

Dm11

Em

Em7

Em9
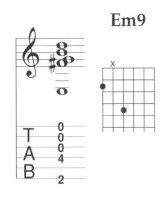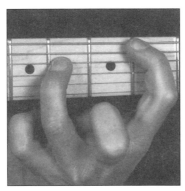

Cm9
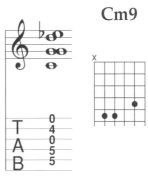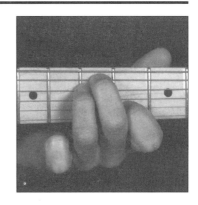

E
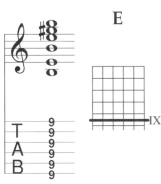

Gmaj7/B
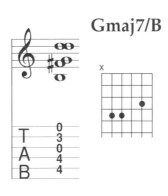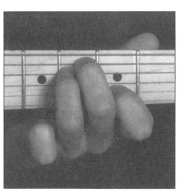

F
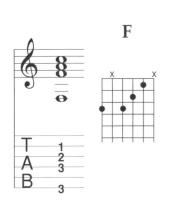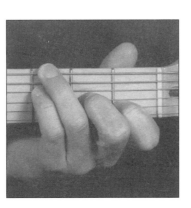

Bb6 add9
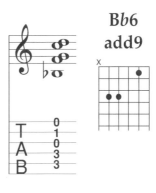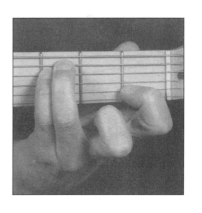

F6/G
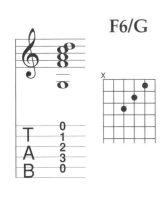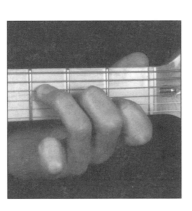

Am11
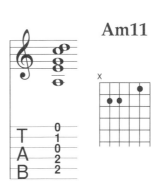

Dm11
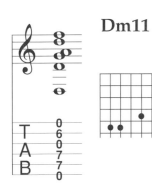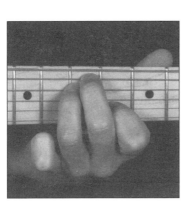

Abmaj7 (add #4)
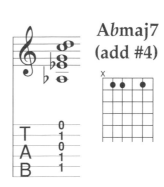

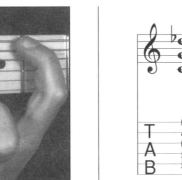

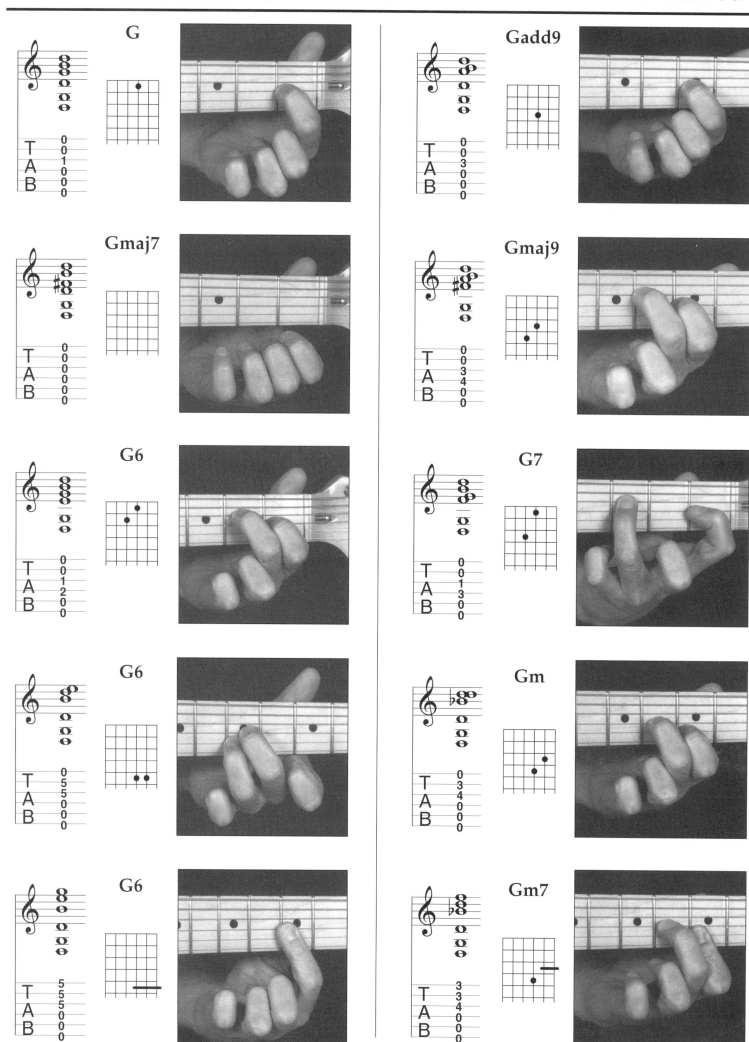

Am11

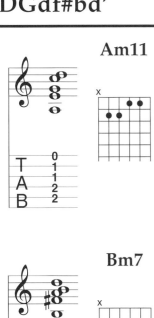

D9

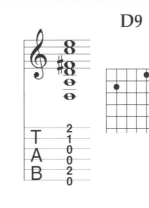

Bm7

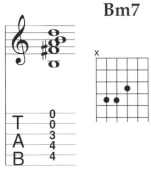

D9

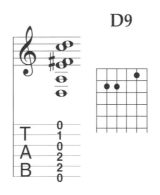
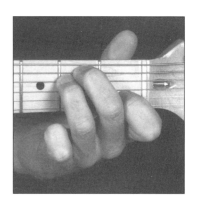

Cadd9/G

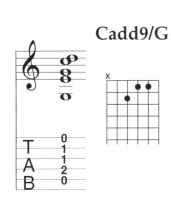

D9

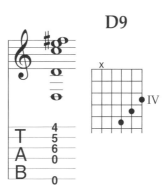
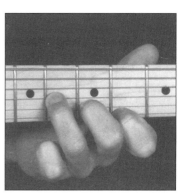

Cm9/G

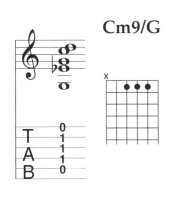

Em7

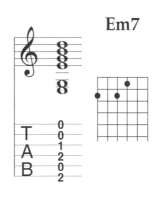
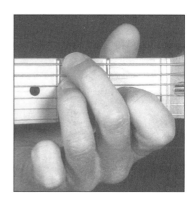

D7

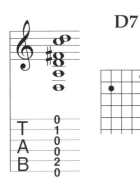
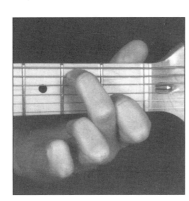

Em9

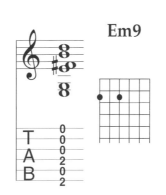
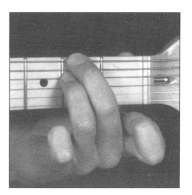

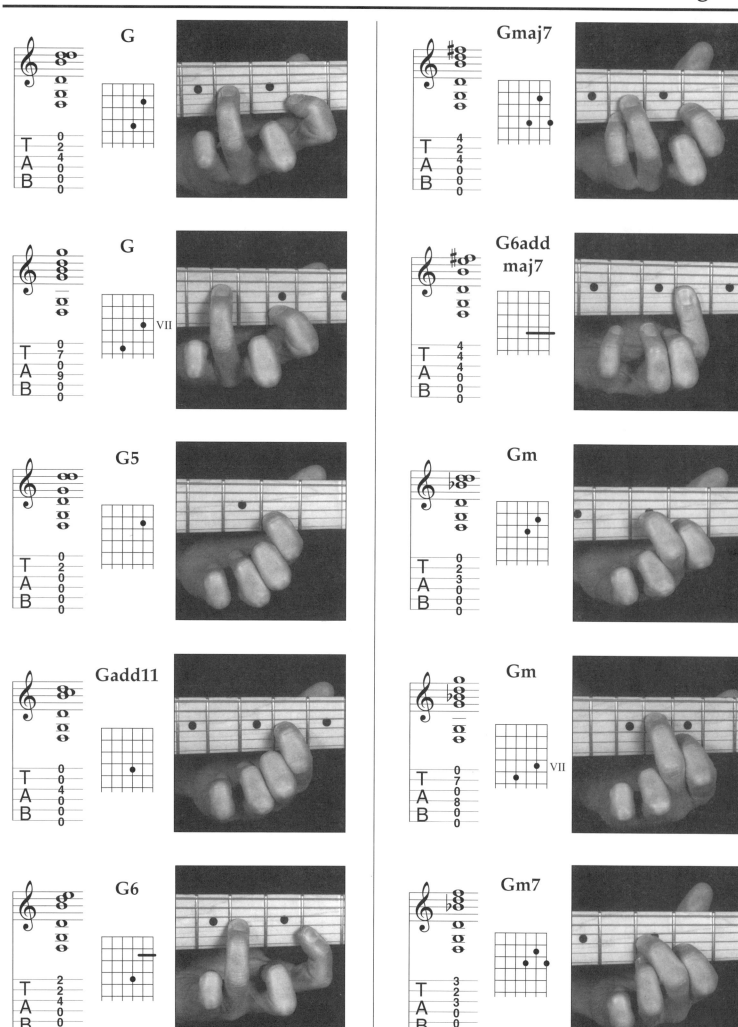

Gm7
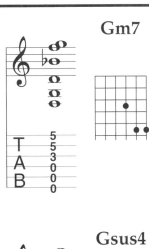
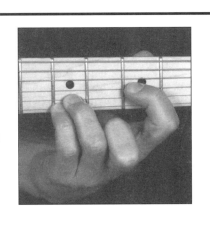

Gsus4
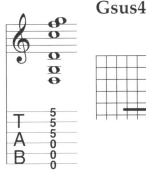
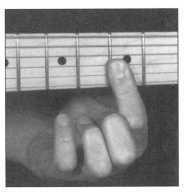

Gm11
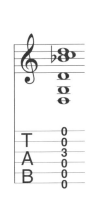
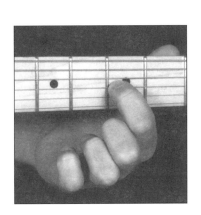

Gm11
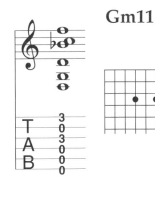
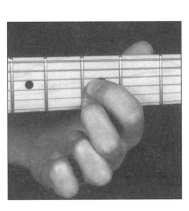

Am11
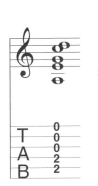
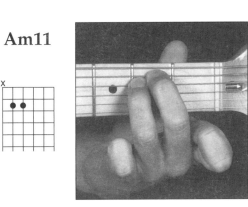

Aadd11
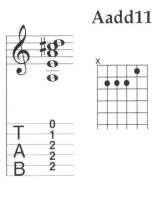
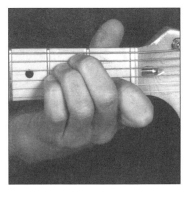

A11
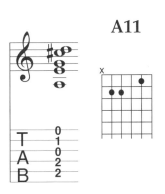
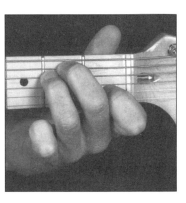

Bbadd9
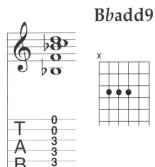

Bbmaj9
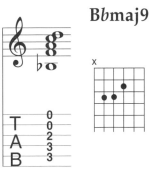

Bm(b9)
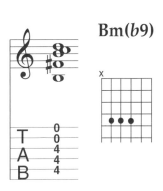
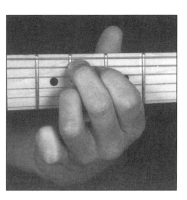

61

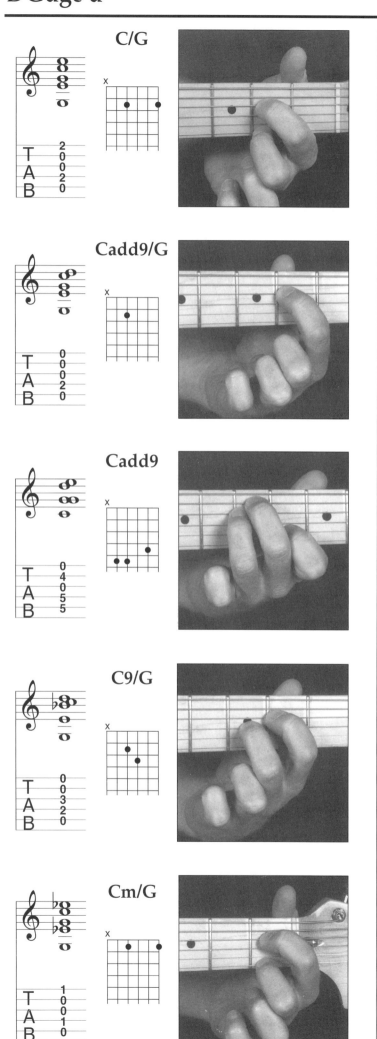

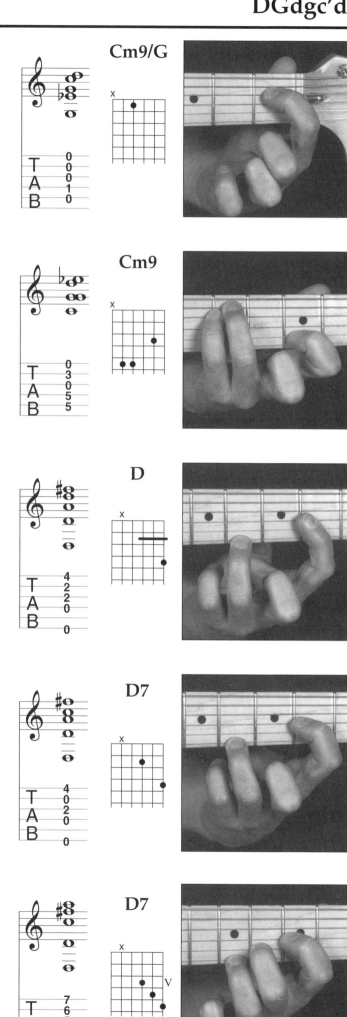

D7

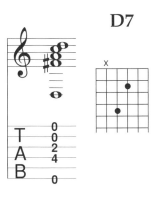
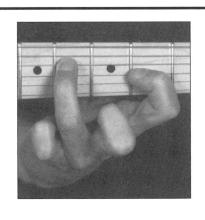

D11

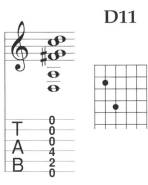

Dm

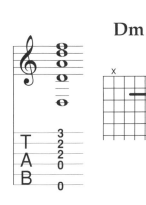
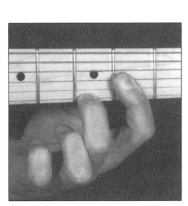

Dm7

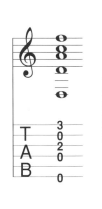
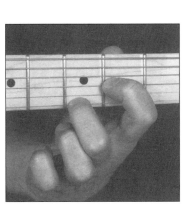

Dm7

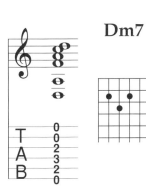
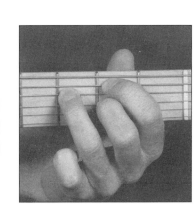

Dm9

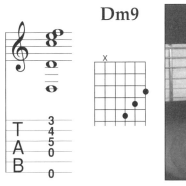
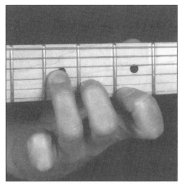

Eb6 add maj7

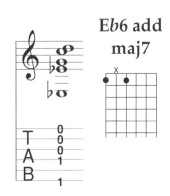

Em7

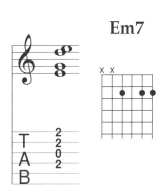
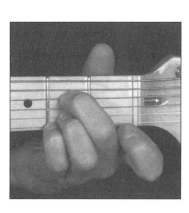

Em7(b6)

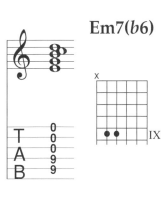
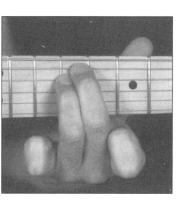

F6

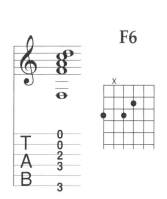
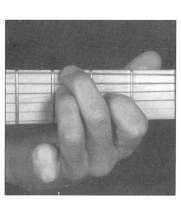

OPEN G-MINOR [DGdgb♭d′]

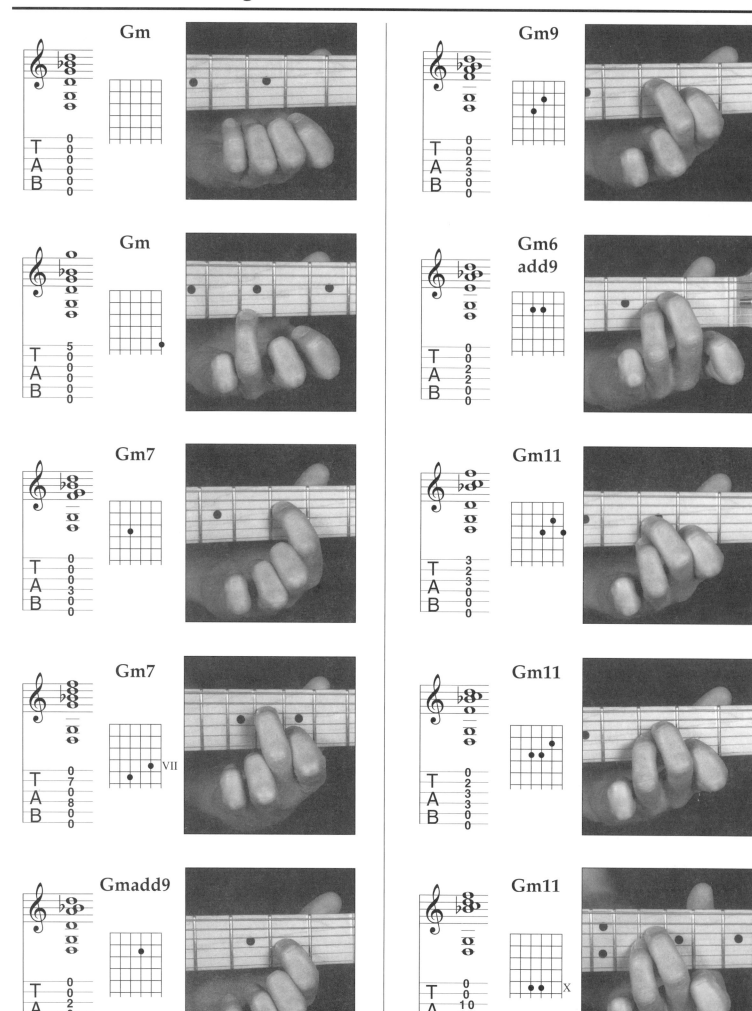

64

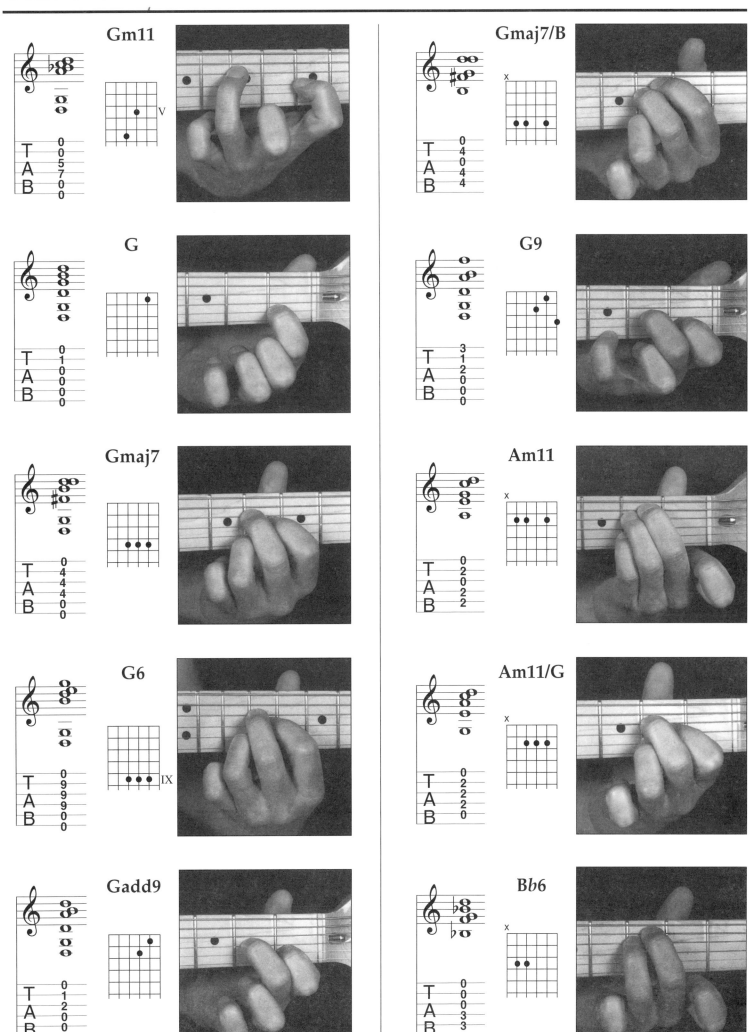

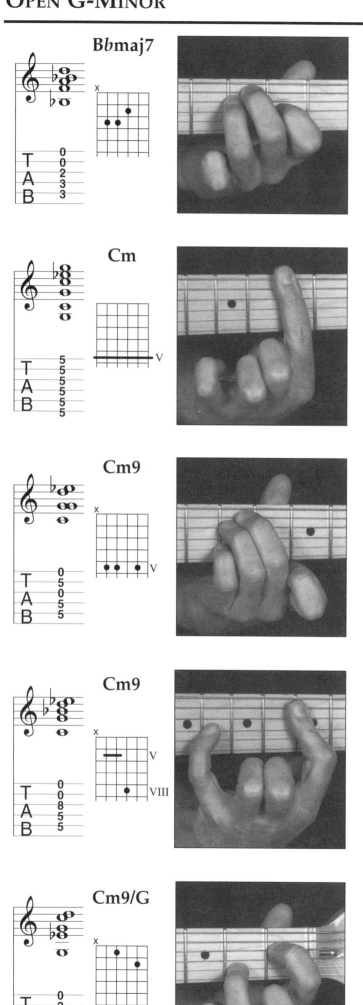

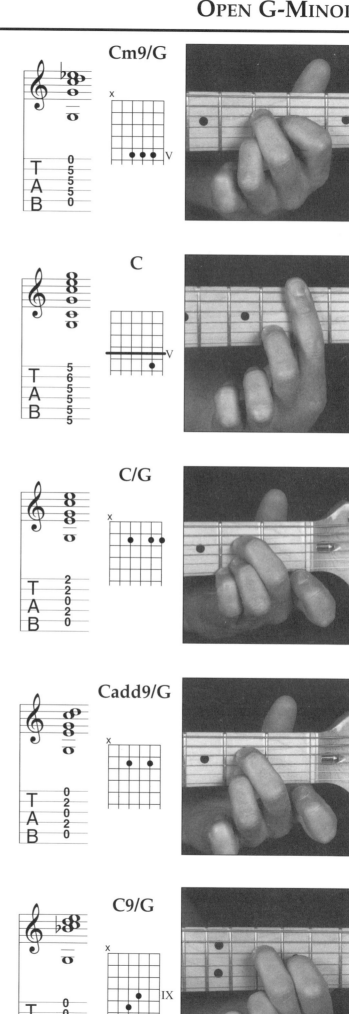

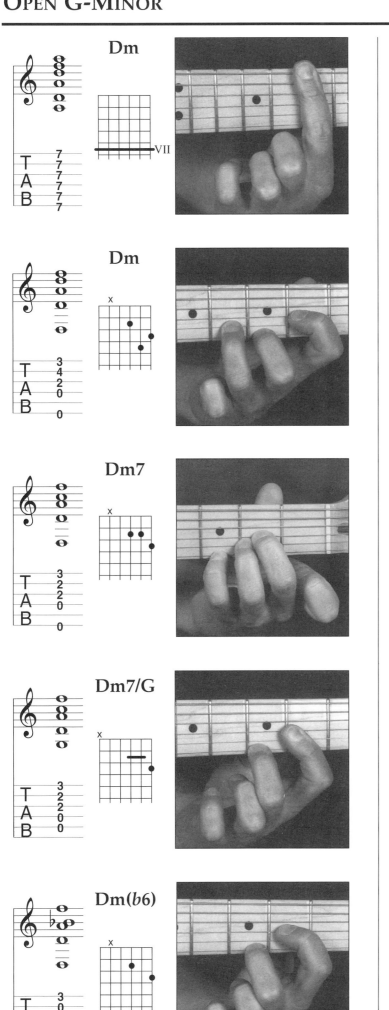

Dm

Dm

Dm7

Dm7/G

Dm(♭6)

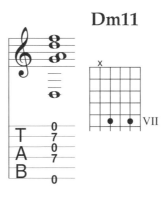

Dm11

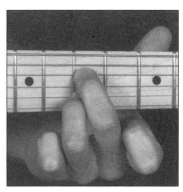

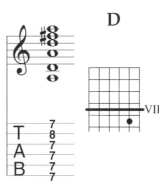

D

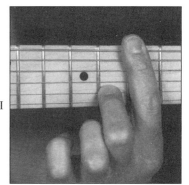

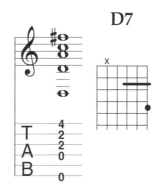

D7

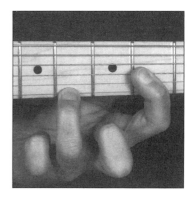

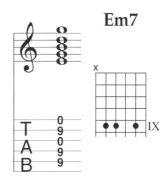

Em7

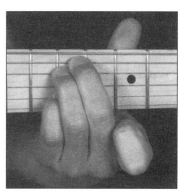

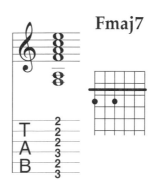

Fmaj7

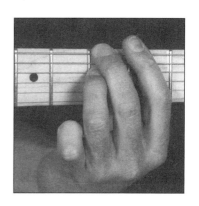

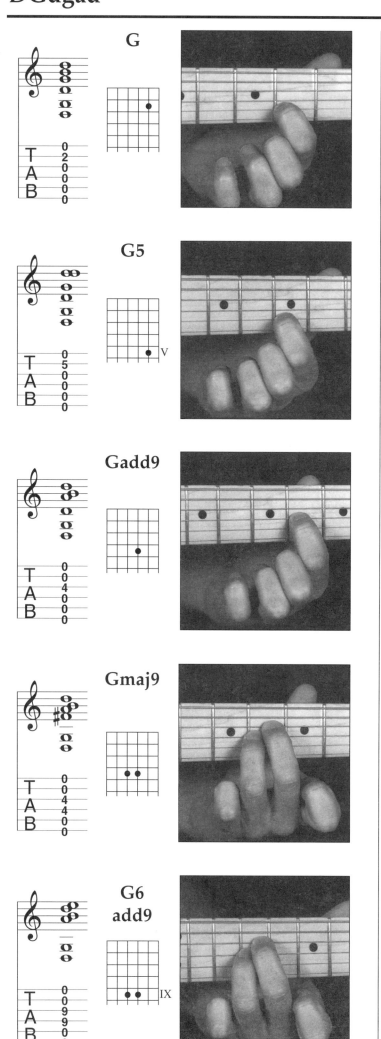

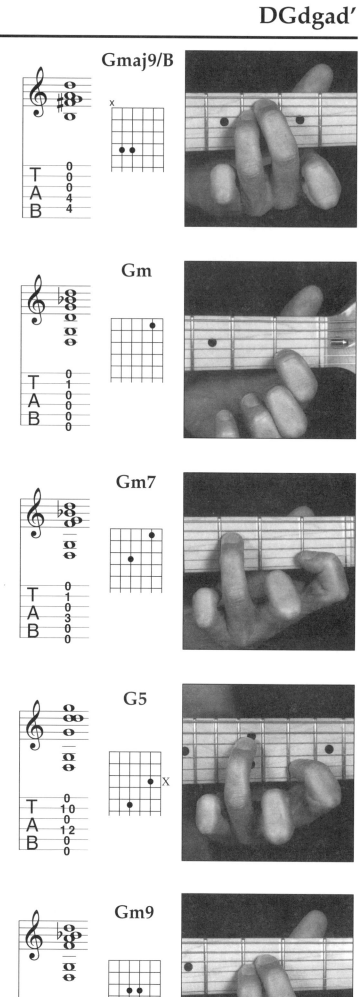

68

Gm11

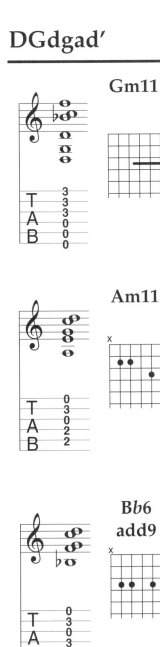

```
T   3
A   3
B   3
    0
    0
```

Am11

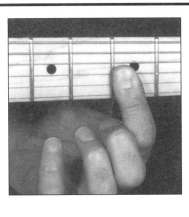

x

```
T   0
A   3
B   2
    2
```

Bb6 add9

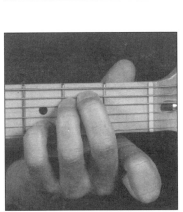

x

```
T   0
A   3
B   0
    3
    3
```

Bbmaj7

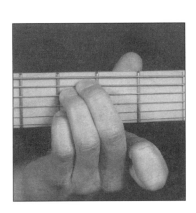

x

```
T   0
A   0
B   3
    3
    3
```

Bm7

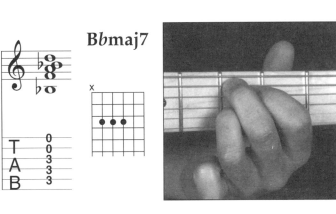

x

```
T   0
A   0
B   4
    4
```

C

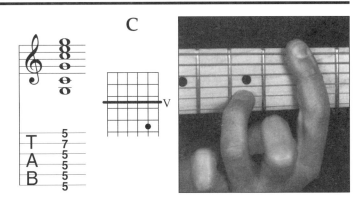

V

```
T   5
A   7
B   5
    5
    5
    5
```

Cadd9/G

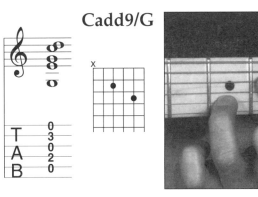

x

```
T   0
A   3
B   0
    2
    0
```

Cm

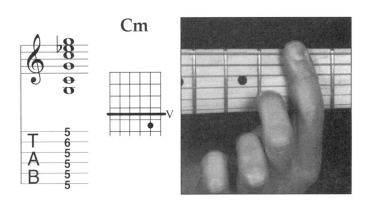

V

```
T   5
A   6
B   5
    5
    5
    5
```

Cm9

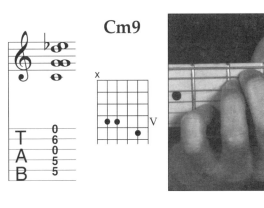

x

V

```
T   0
A   6
B   0
    5
    5
```

Cm9/G

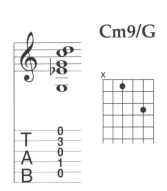

x

```
T   0
A   3
B   0
    1
    0
```

D

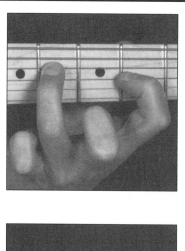

Dadd11

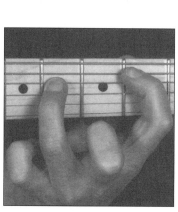

D7

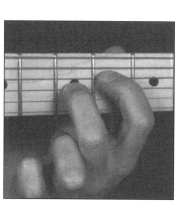

Dm

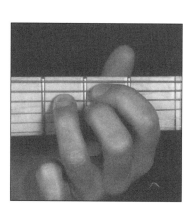

Dm11

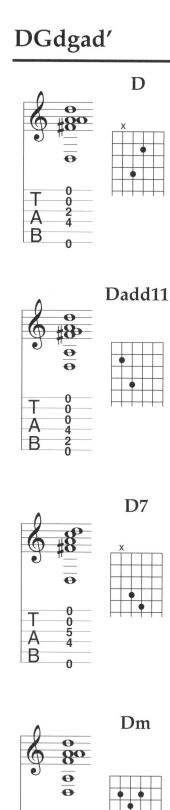
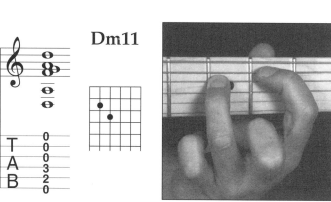

Ebmaj7

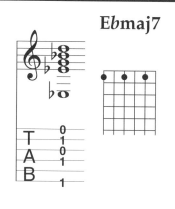

Em11

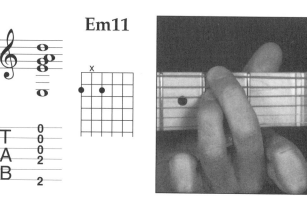

E7

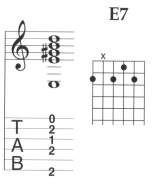

F6

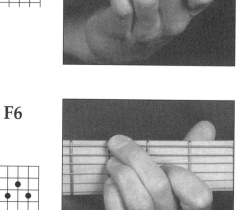

F#m(b6)

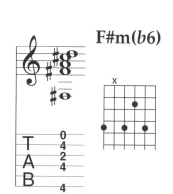
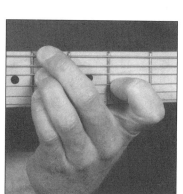

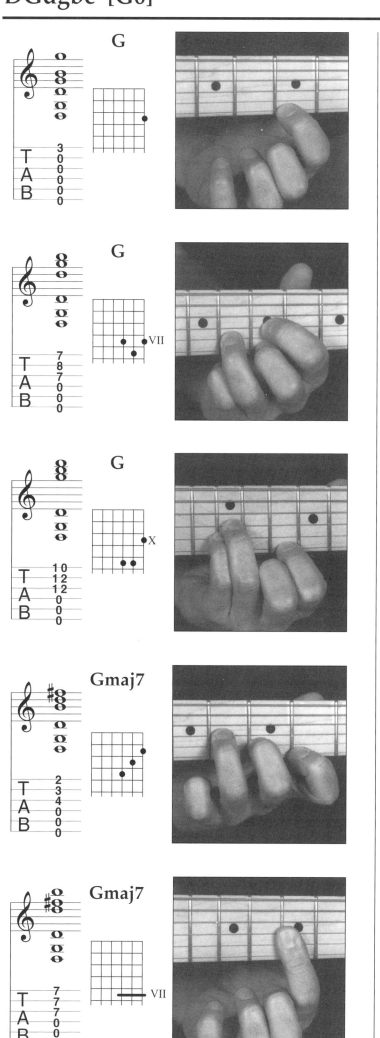
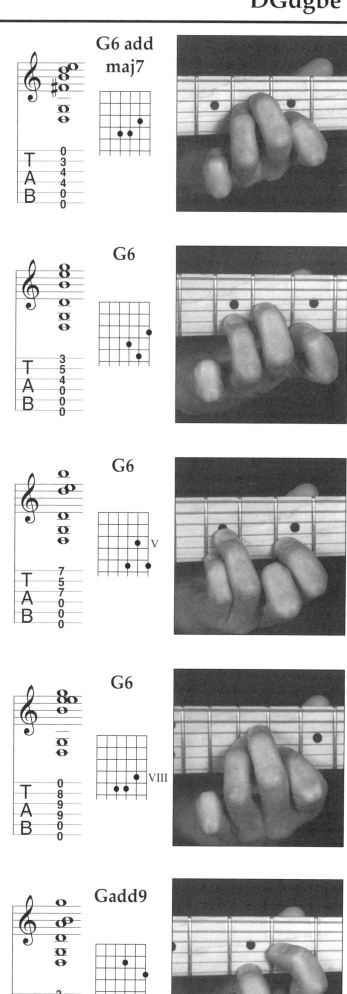

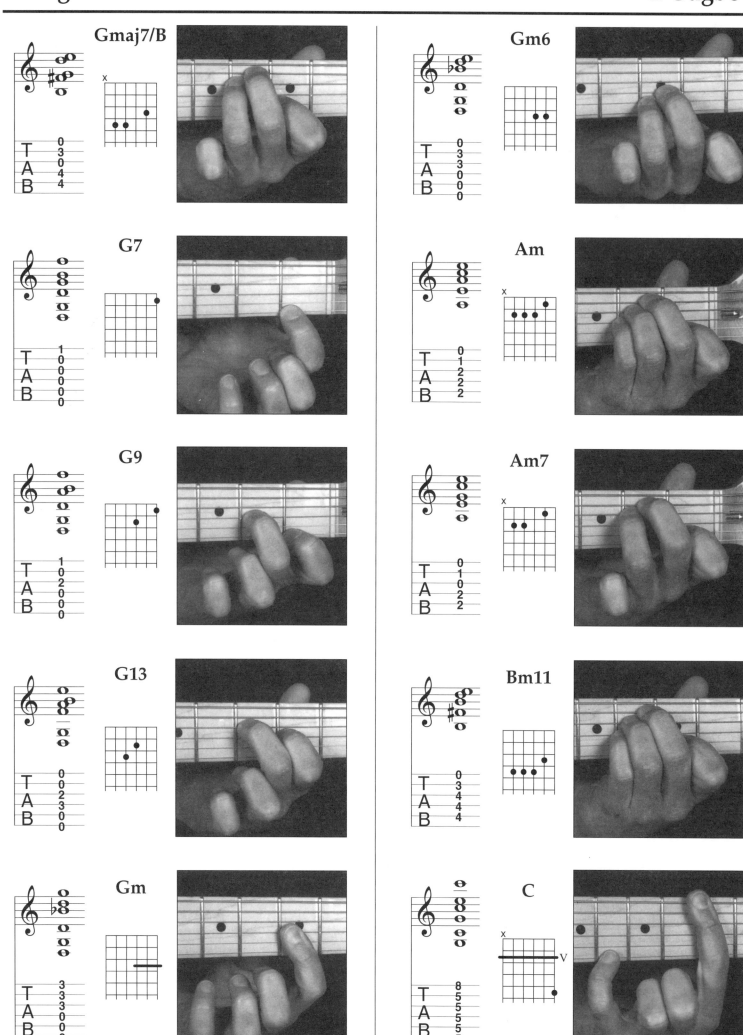

C/G

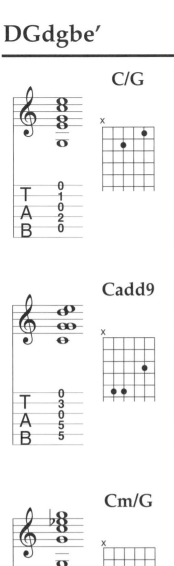

Cadd9

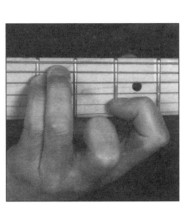

Cm/G

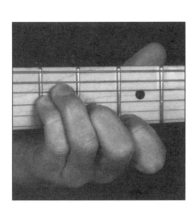

D

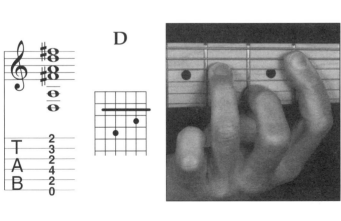

D7

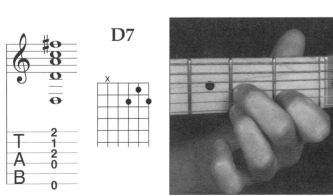

D9

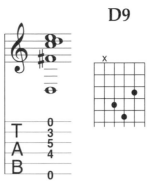

D9

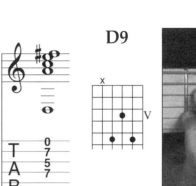

Em

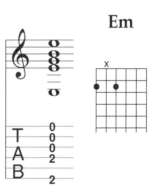

Em9

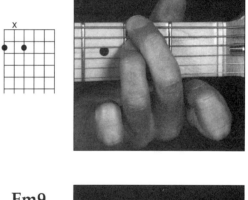

Fmaj7

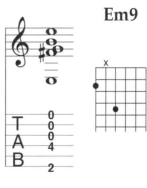

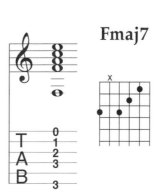

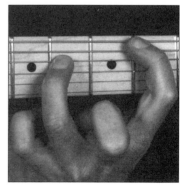

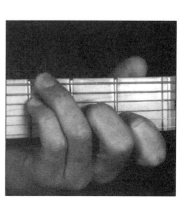

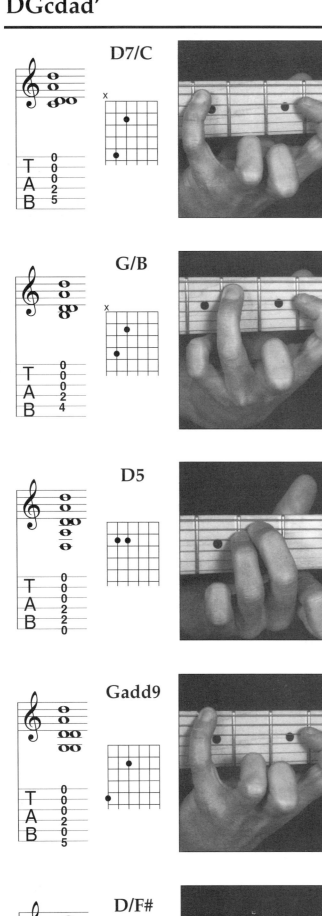

D7/C

G/B

D5

Gadd9

D/F#

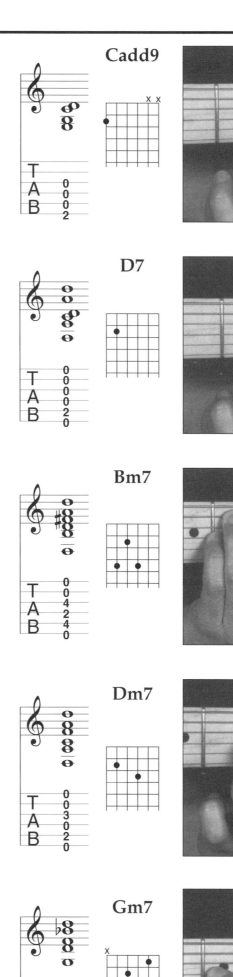

Cadd9

D7

Bm7

Dm7

Gm7

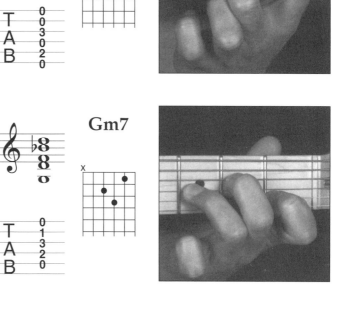

Collings SJ

Taylor 914-C

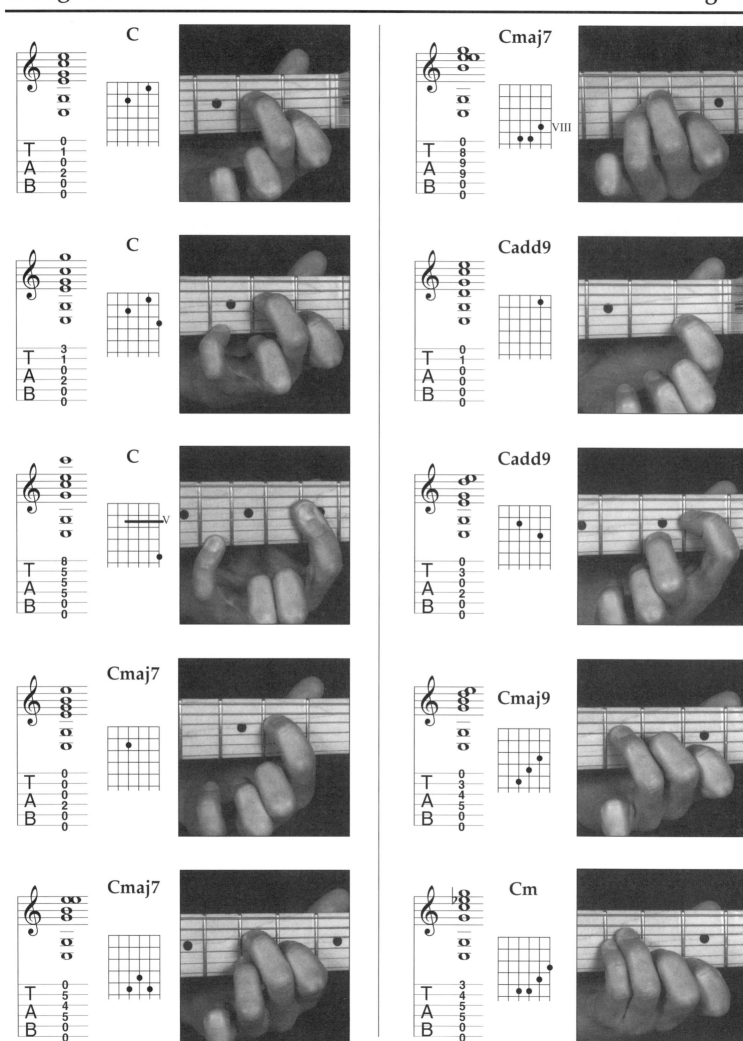

CGdgbe'

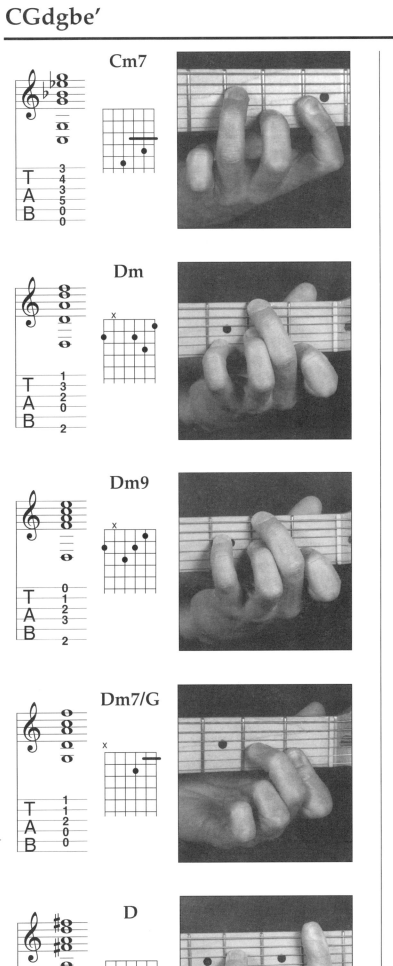
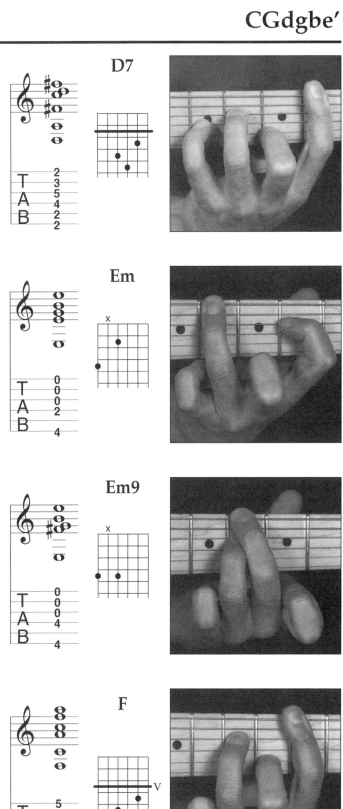

Cm7

Dm

Dm9

Dm7/G

D

D7

Em

Em9

F

Fmaj7/G

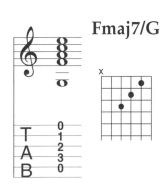
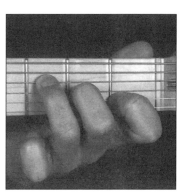

77

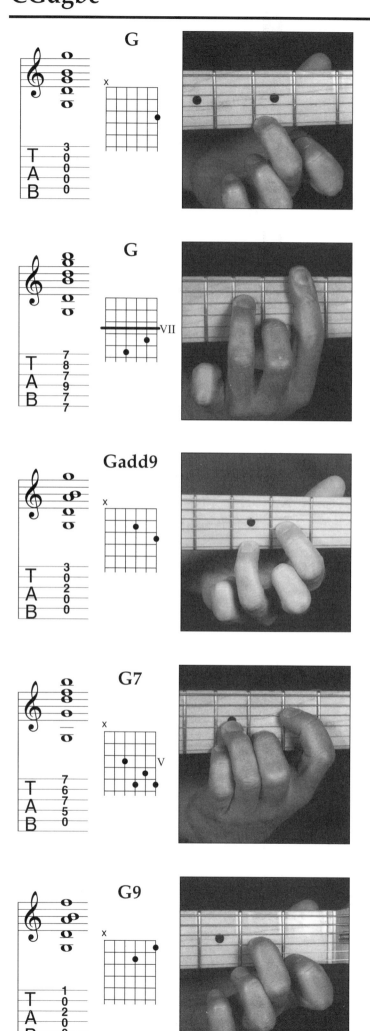
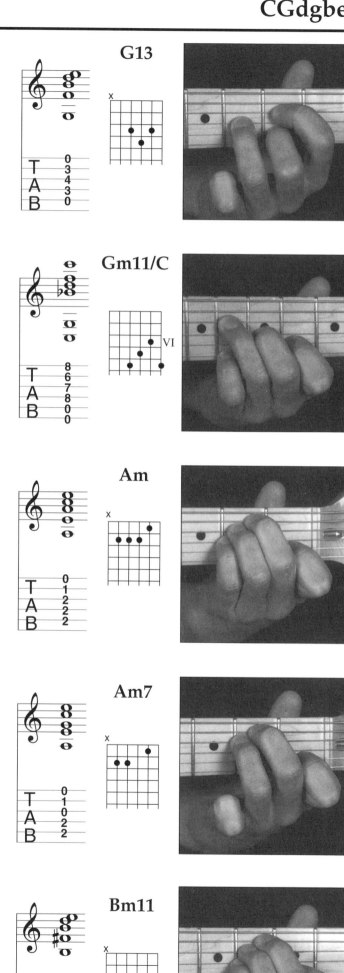

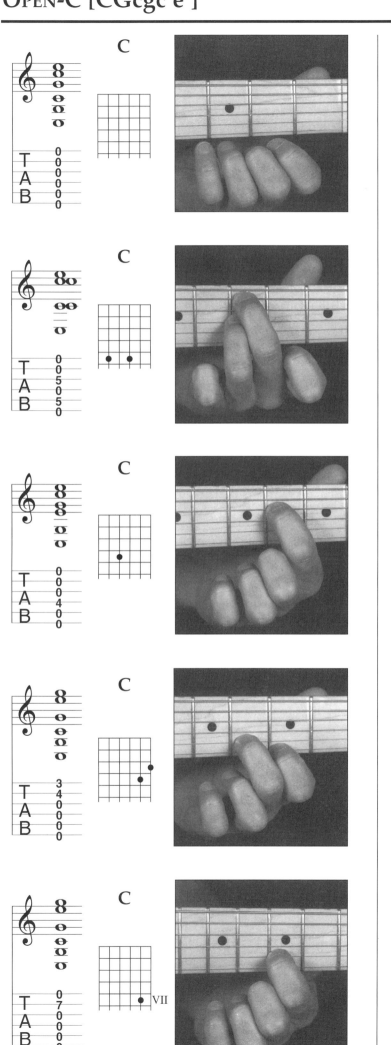
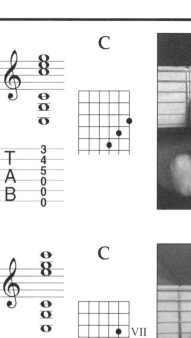
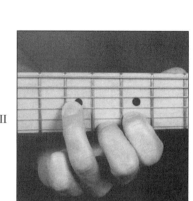
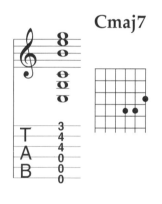
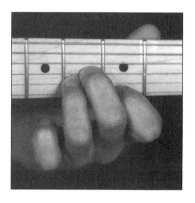
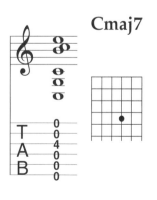
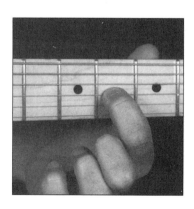
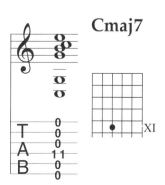
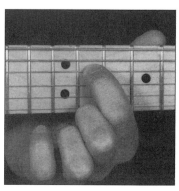

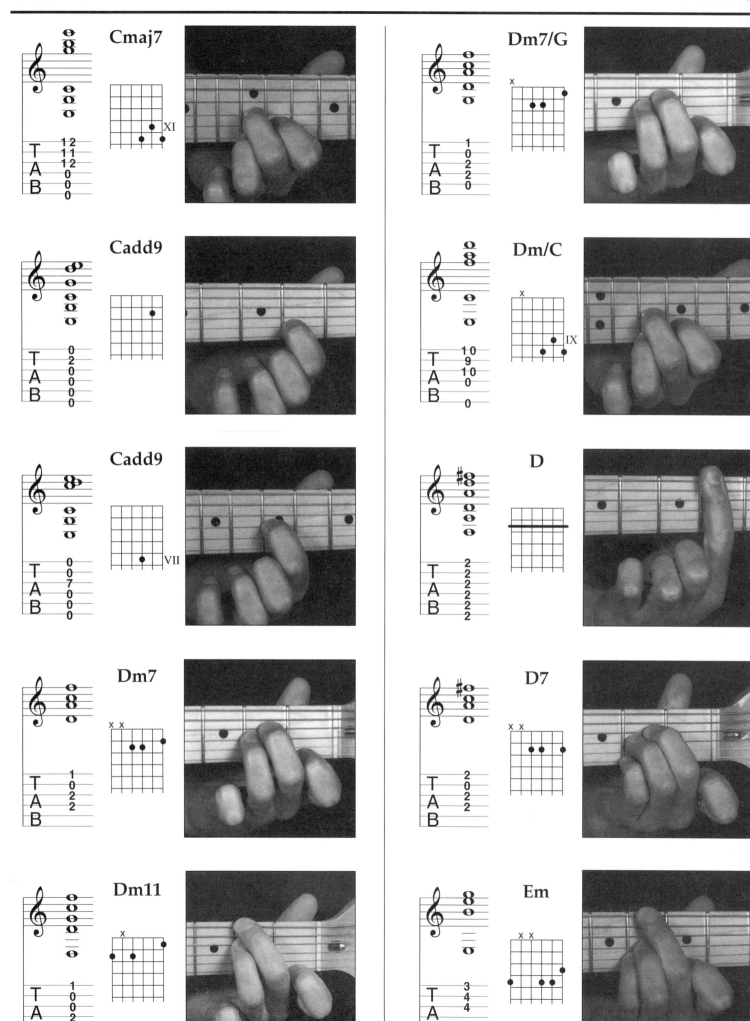

Cmaj7

Cadd9

Cadd9

Dm7

Dm11

Dm7/G

Dm/C

D

D7

Em

Em7

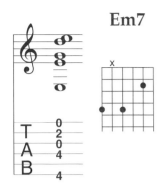

```
T  0
A  2
B  0
   4
   4
```

G

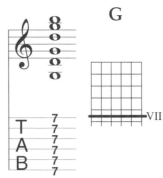
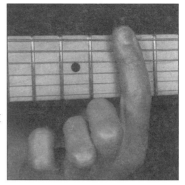

```
T  7
A  7
B  7
   7
   7
```
VII

F

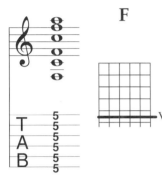
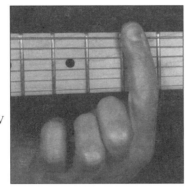

```
T  5
A  5
B  5
   5
   5
   5
```
V

G6 (no3rd)

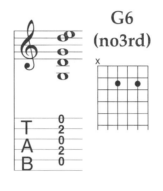

```
T  0
A  2
B  0
   2
   0
```

Fadd9

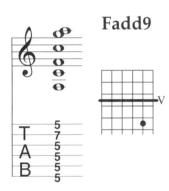
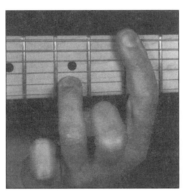

```
T  5
A  7
B  5
   5
   5
   5
```
V

G6 add11

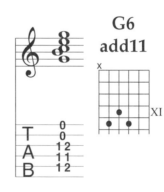

```
T  0
A  0
B  12
   11
   12
```
XI

F/C

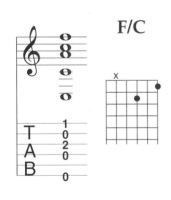
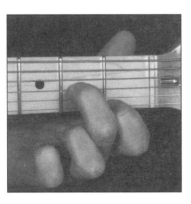

```
T  1
A  0
B  2
   0
   0
```

Am

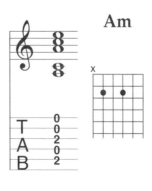
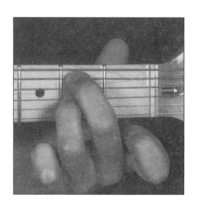

```
T  0
A  0
B  2
   0
   2
```

Fmaj7

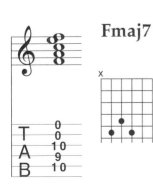
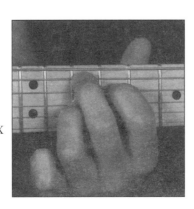

```
T  0
A  0
B  10
   9
   10
```
IX

Am9

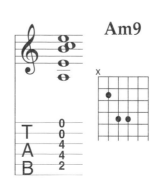
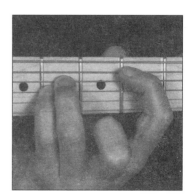

```
T  0
A  0
B  4
   2
```

81

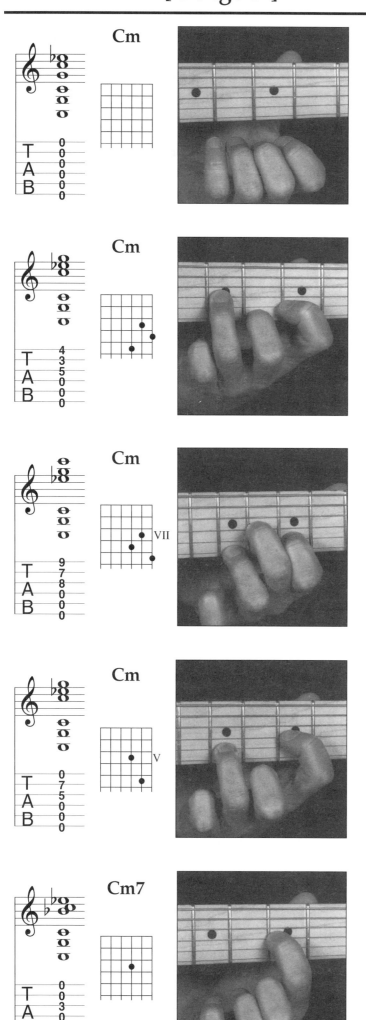

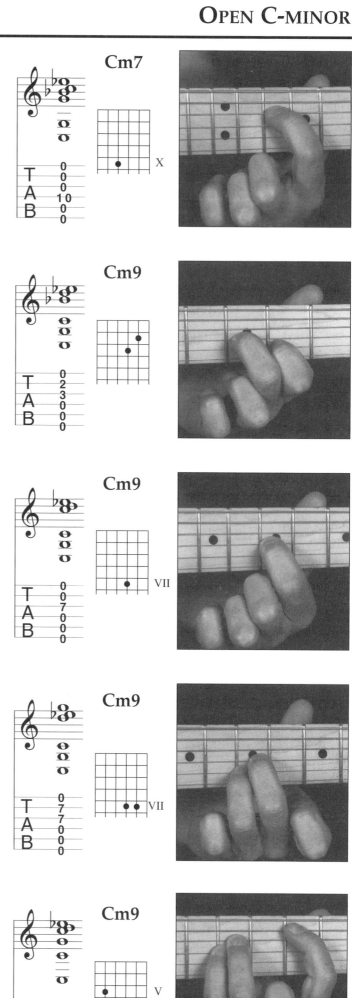

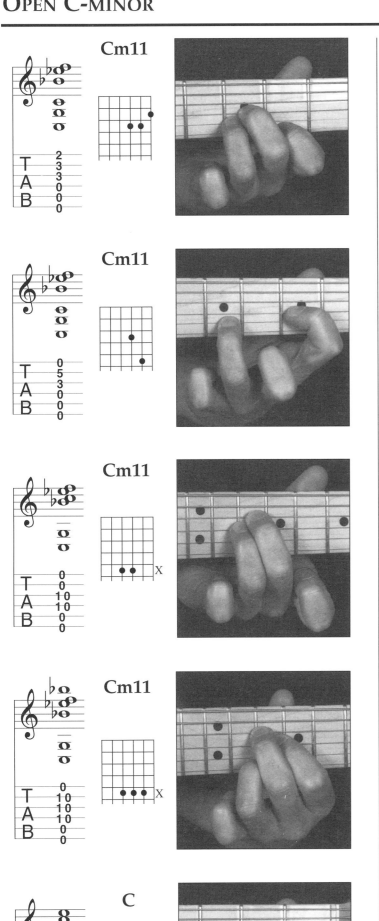
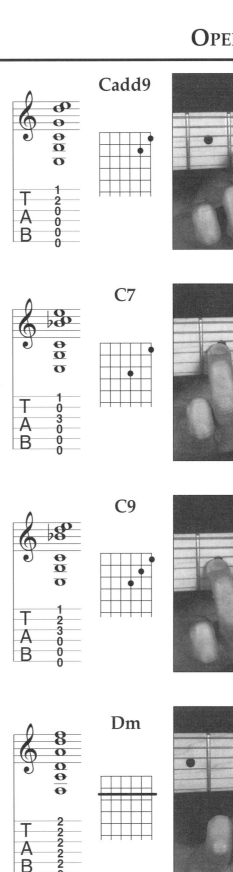
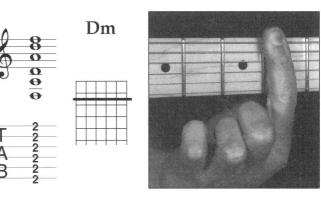
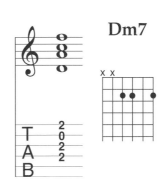
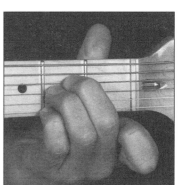

Dm7/G

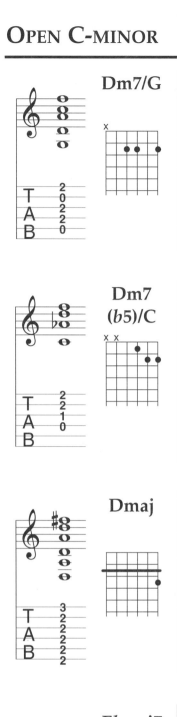
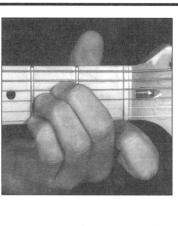

Dm7 (b5)/C

Dmaj

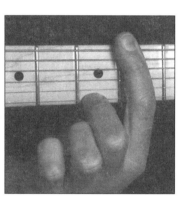

Ebmaj7 /Bb

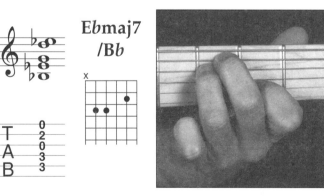

Ebmaj7/G

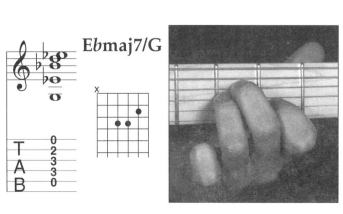

Fm

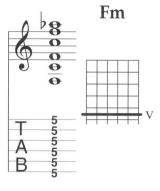

Fm7

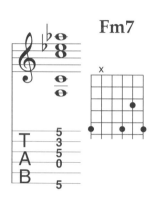
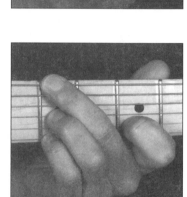

Fm9

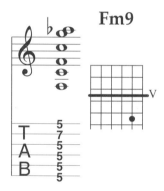
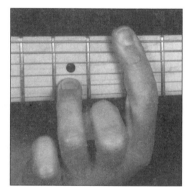

Gm

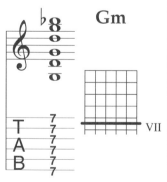
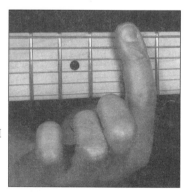

Gm(b6)

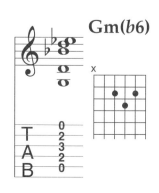
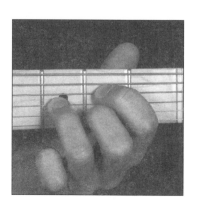

Gm11
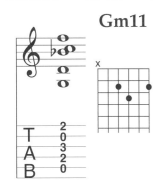
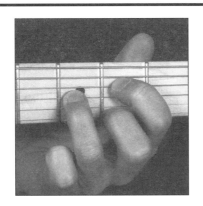

Abmaj7
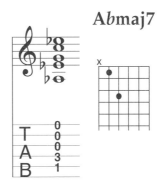
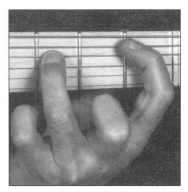

G
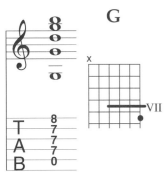

Abadd9
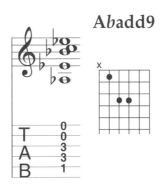
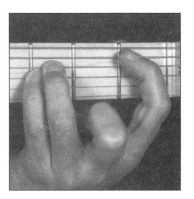

Gadd11
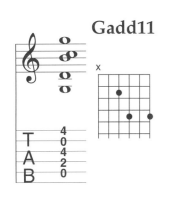
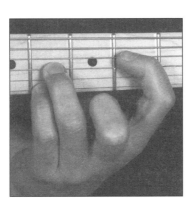

Bb
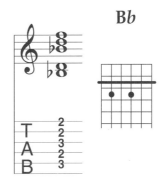
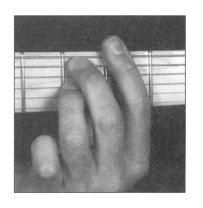

G7
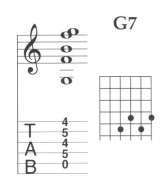

Bbadd9 add11
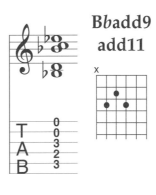
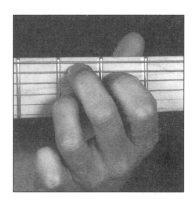

Ab
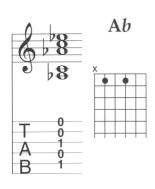
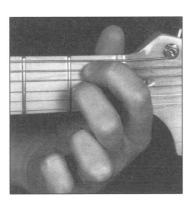

Bbsus4 add9
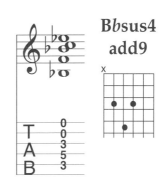

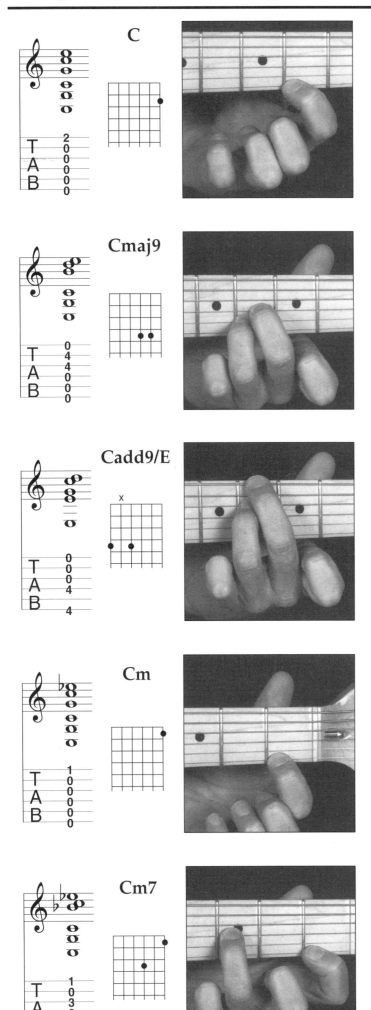

C

Cmaj9

Cadd9/E

Cm

Cm7

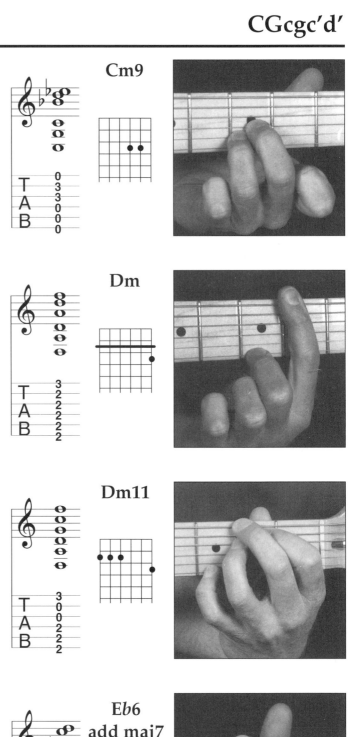

Cm9

Dm

Dm11

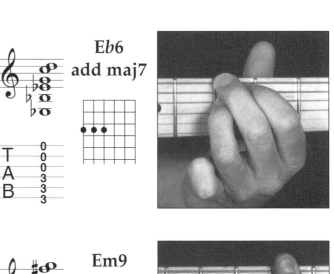

Eb6
add maj7

Em9

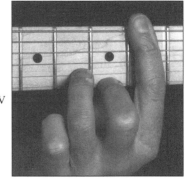

F

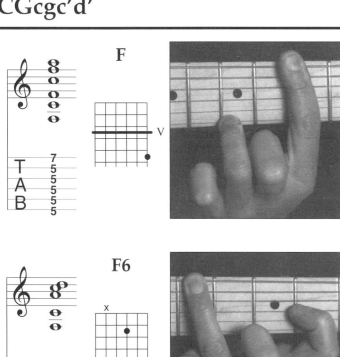

F6

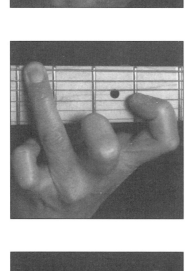

Fadd9

G

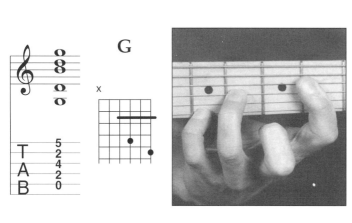

Gadd11

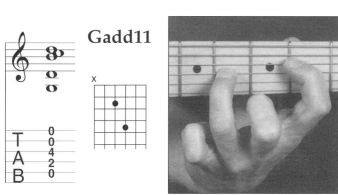

G/B add11

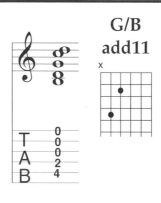

Gm11

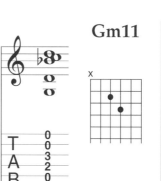

Am7

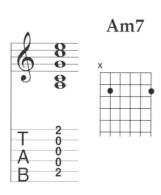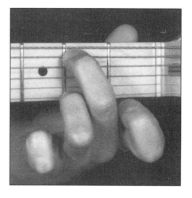

Am11

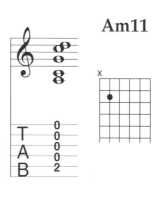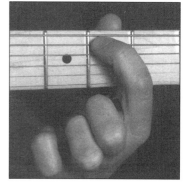

Bb6 add9

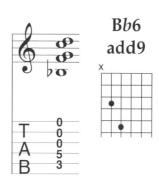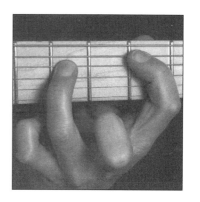

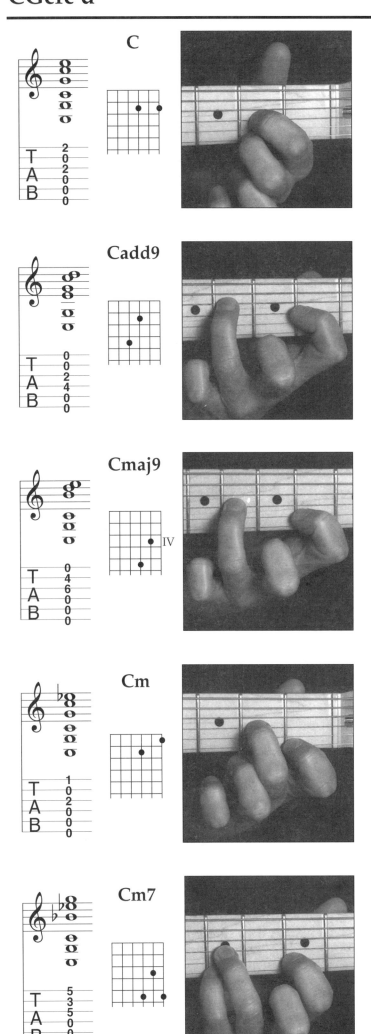

C

Cadd9

Cmaj9

Cm

Cm7

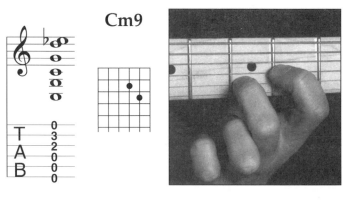

Cm9

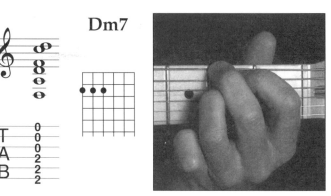

Dm7

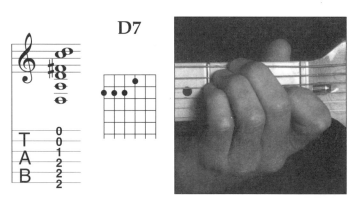

D7

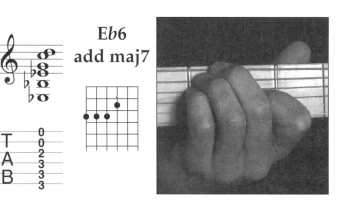

Eb6
add maj7

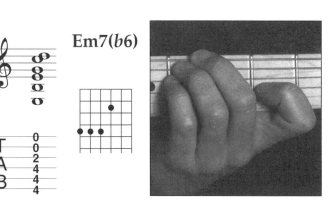

Em7(b6)

F6

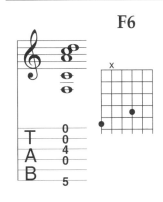
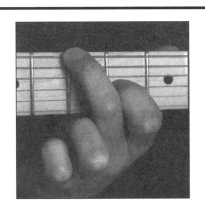

Gadd11

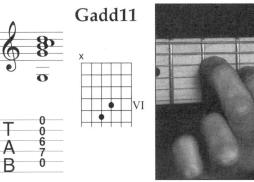

F6

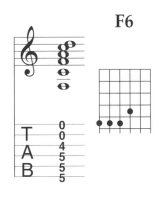
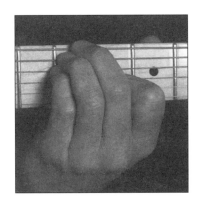

Gm11

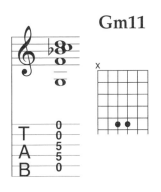
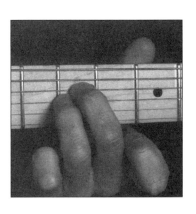

G

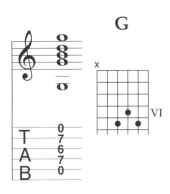
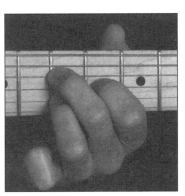

Am11

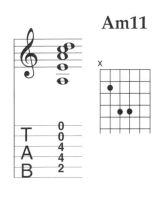
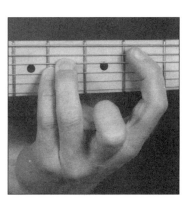

Gsus4

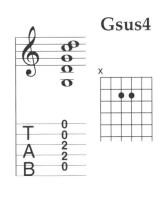
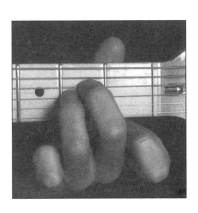

Am11

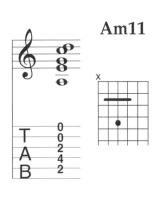

G11

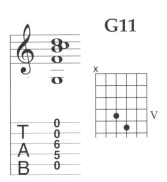
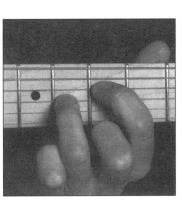

Bbadd9

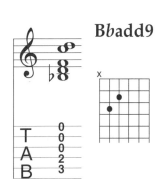

89

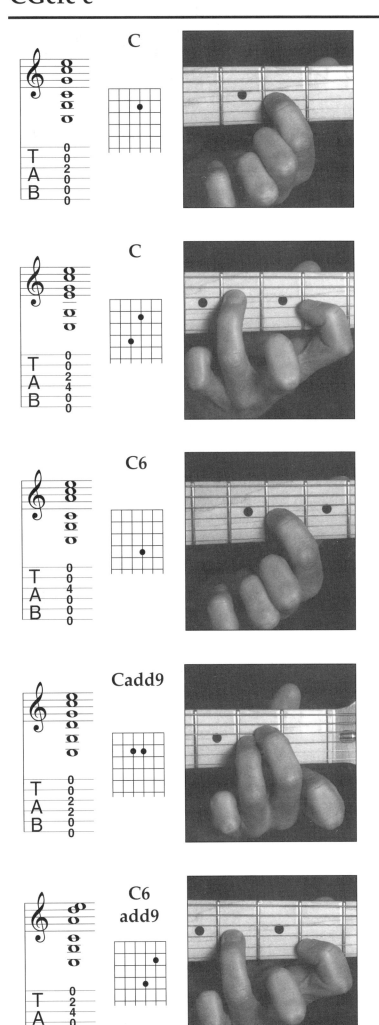

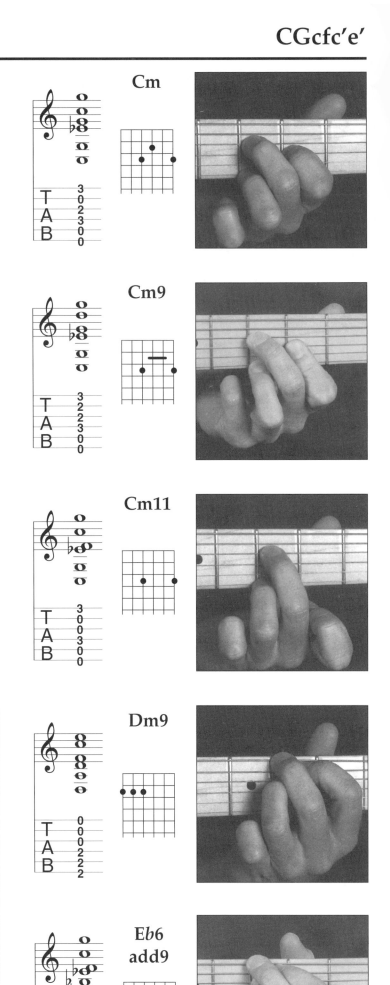

90

CGcfc′e′

Em(b6)
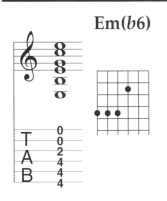
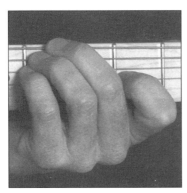

G13sus4
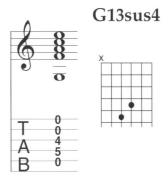
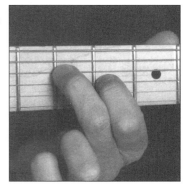

F
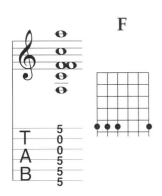
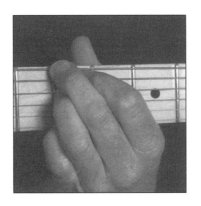

Gm9
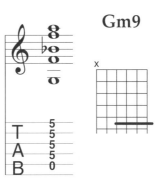
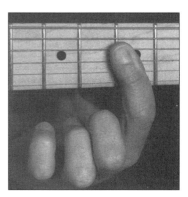

Fmaj7
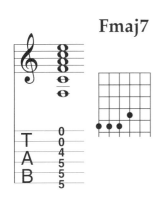
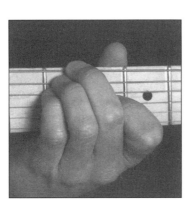

Am7
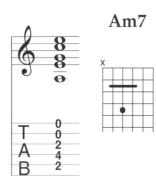

G
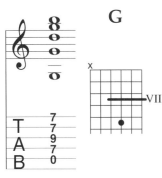
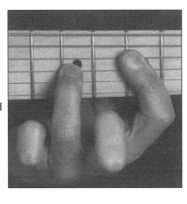

Am(b6)
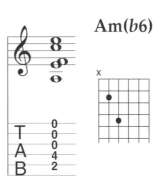

G13
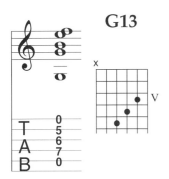

Bbadd9
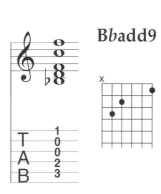
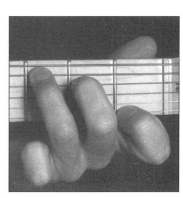

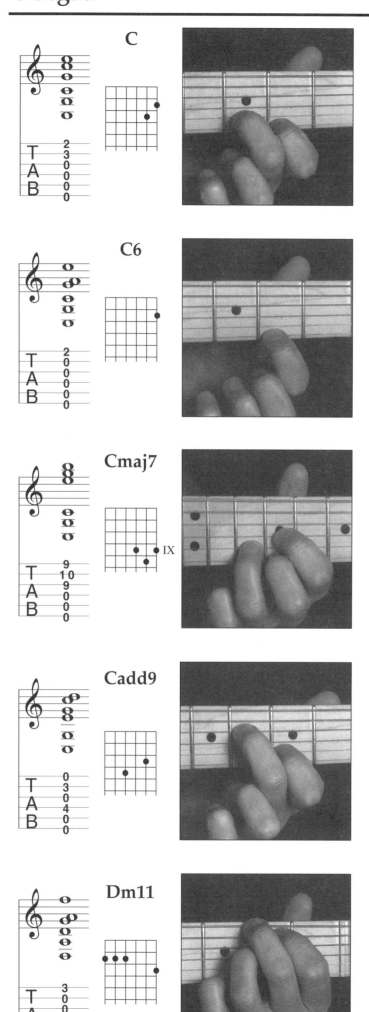

C

C6

Cmaj7

IX

Cadd9

Dm11

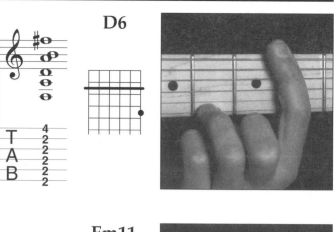

D6

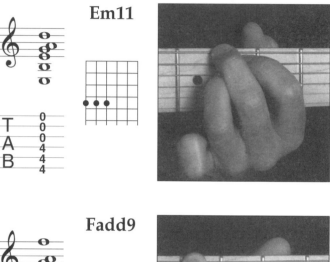

Em11

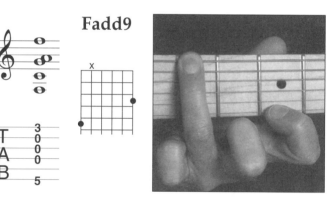

Fadd9

x

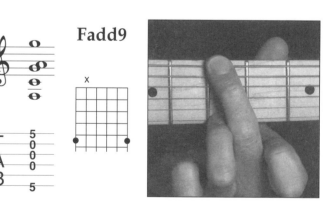

Fadd9

x

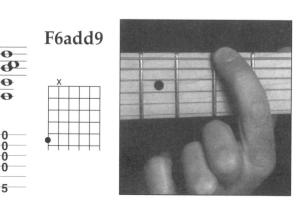

F6add9

x

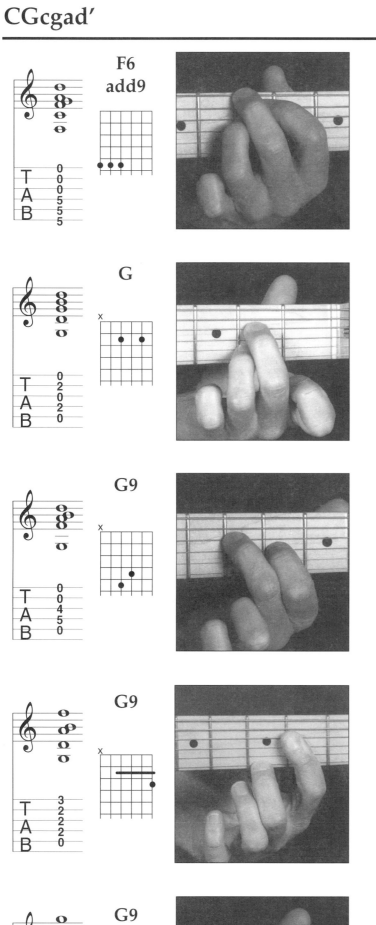

F6 add9

G

G9

G9

G9

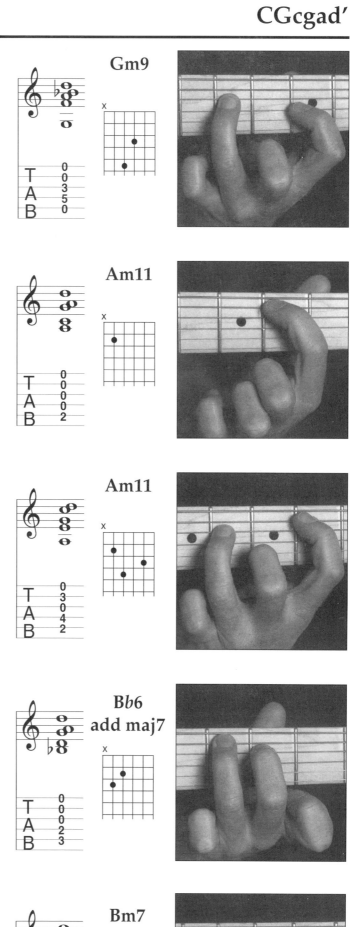

Gm9

Am11

Am11

Bb6 add maj7

Bm7

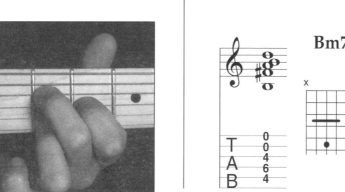

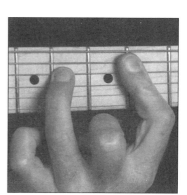

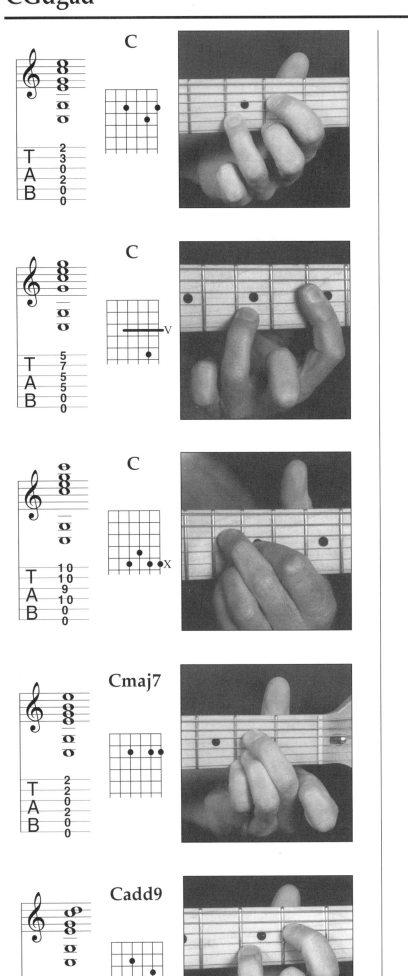
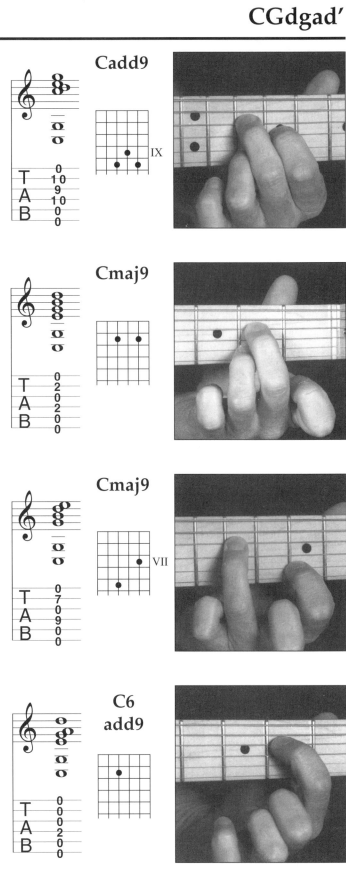

C

C

C

Cmaj7

Cadd9

Cadd9

Cmaj9

Cmaj9

C6
add9

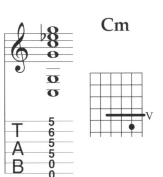
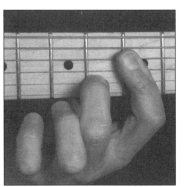

Cm

Cm9
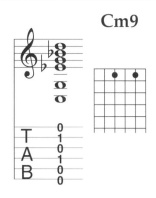
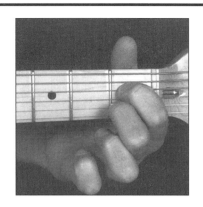

D6 add9
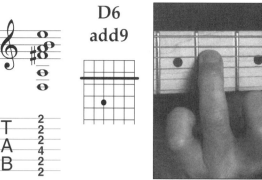
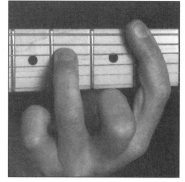

Cm9
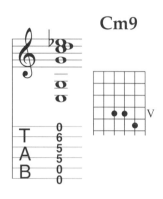

Dadd11
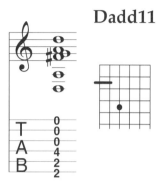
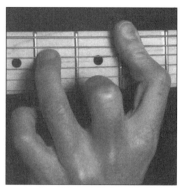

Cm11
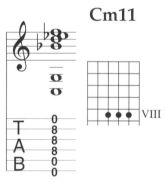
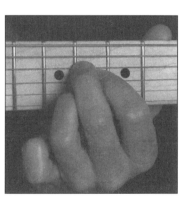

Ebmaj7
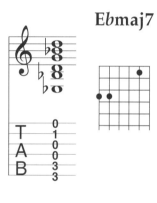

Dm
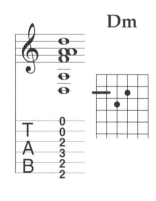

Em7
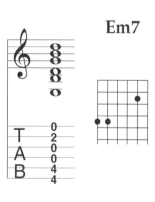
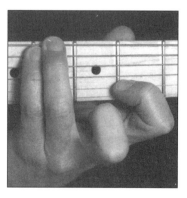

Dm11
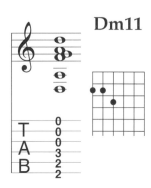
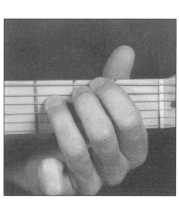

Em11
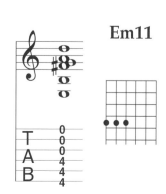
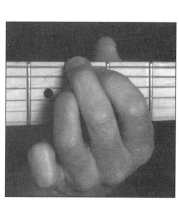

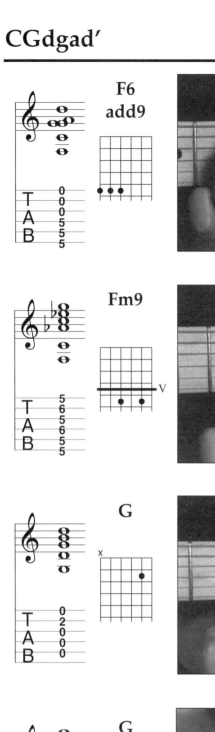
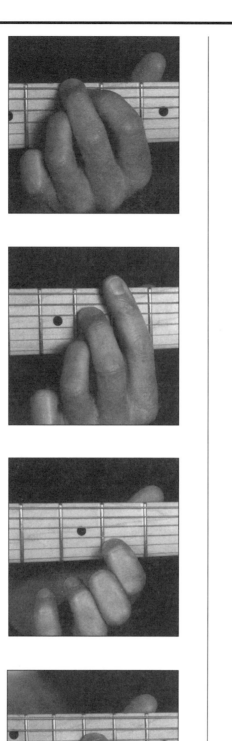
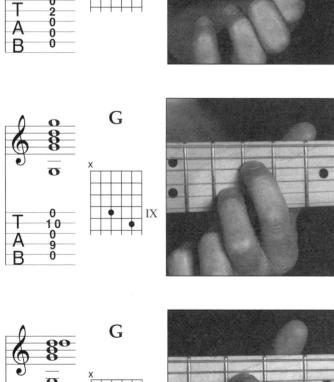
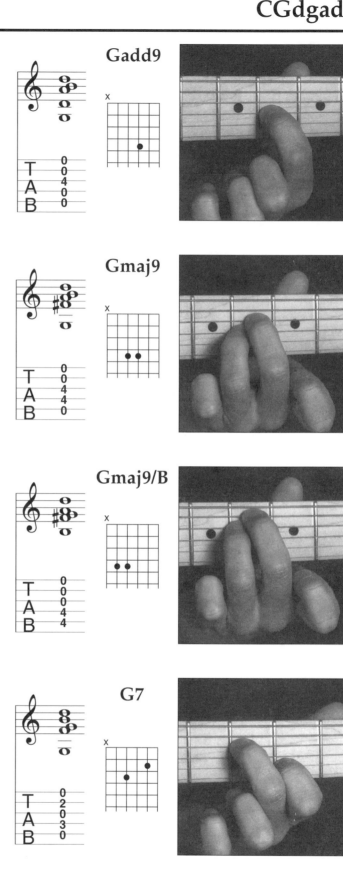
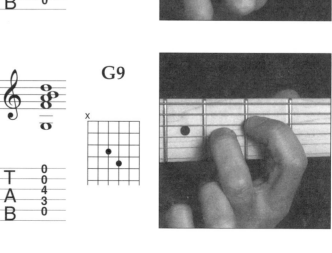

Gm

```
T  0
A  1
B  0
   0
   0
```

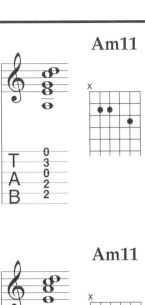

Am11

```
T  0
A  3
B  0
   2
   2
```

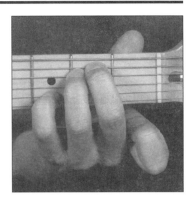

Gm9

```
T  0
A  0
B  3
   0
```

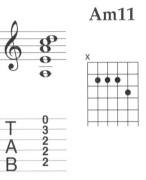

Am11

```
T  0
A  3
B  2
   2
   2
```

Gm9

```
T  0
A  0
B  3
   3
   0
```

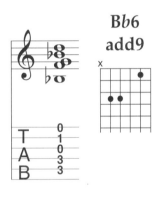

Bb6 add9

```
T  0
A  1
B  0
   3
   3
```

Gm11

```
T  3
A  3
B  3
   0
   0
```

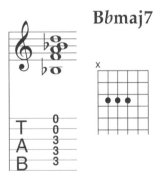

Bbmaj7

```
T  0
A  0
B  3
   3
   3
```

Gm11

```
T  0
A  3
B  3
   3
   0
```

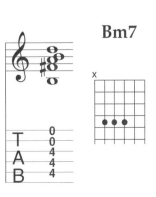

Bm7

```
T  0
A  0
B  4
   4
   4
```

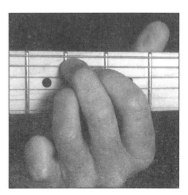

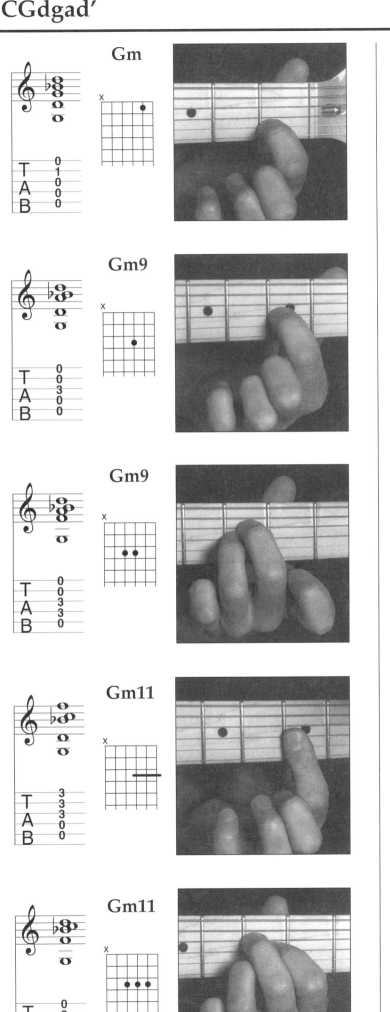

CGdgbd′ [Open-G with C Bass]

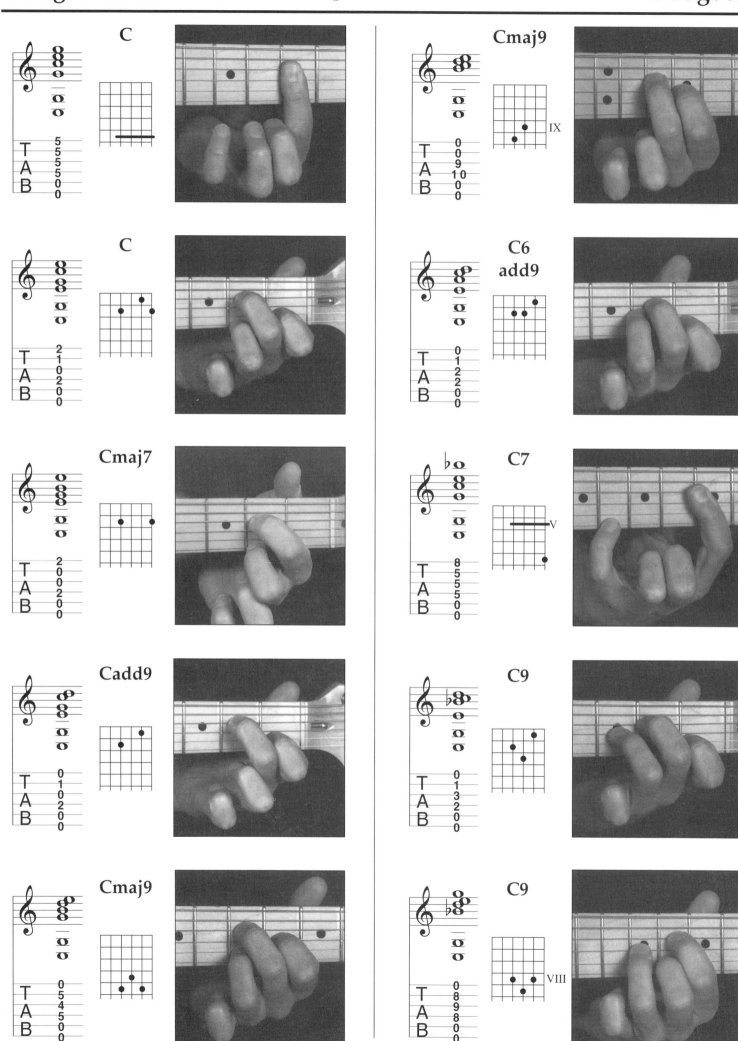

Cm
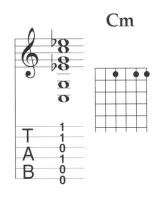

D
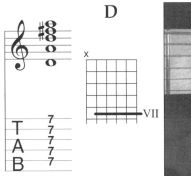
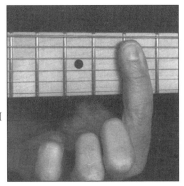

Cm9
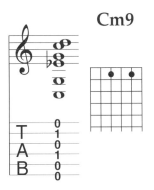

D
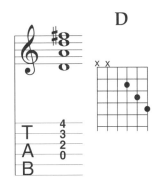

Cm9
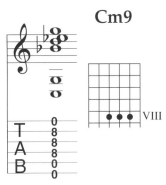
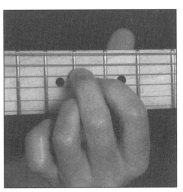

Dm11
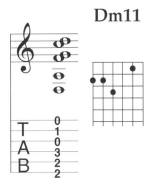
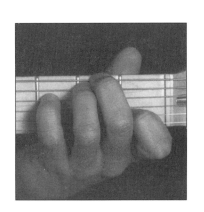

Cm6 add9
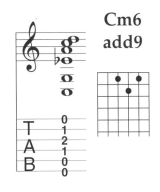

Eb6 add maj7
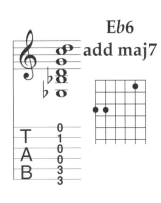
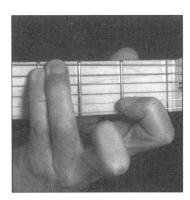

Cm11
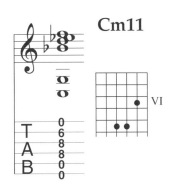
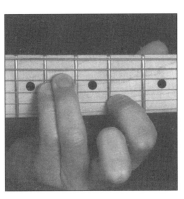

Ebmaj7
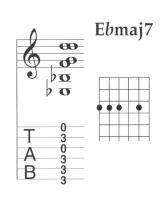
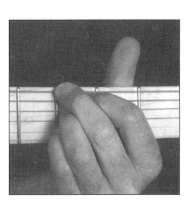

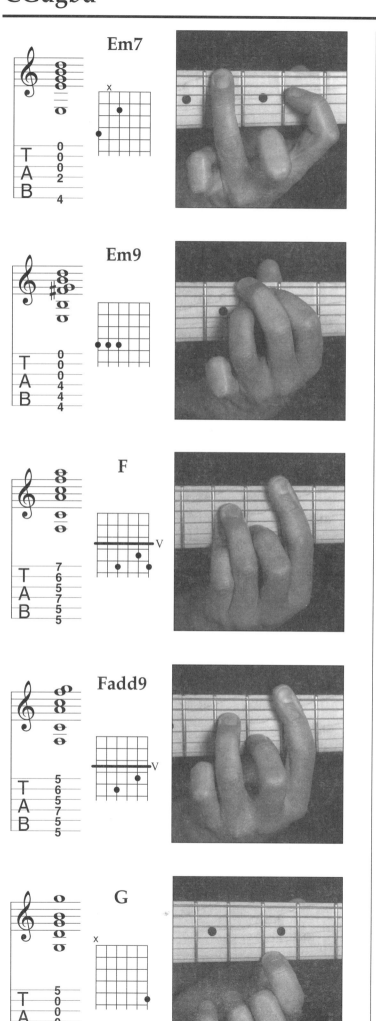

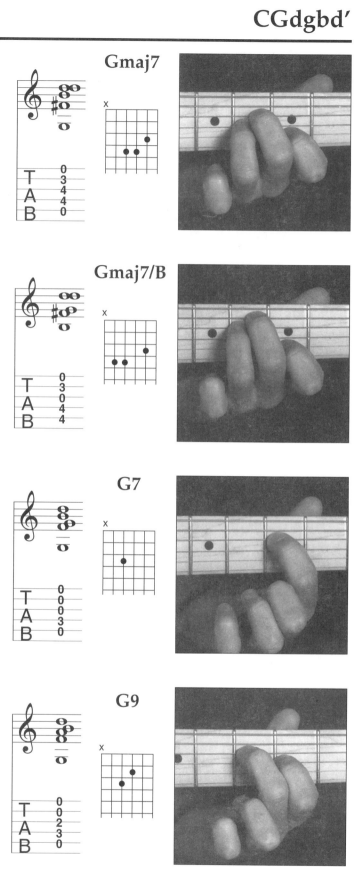

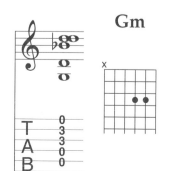

Gm7

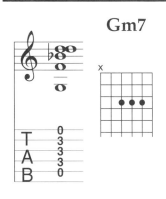

Am11

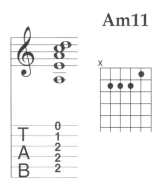

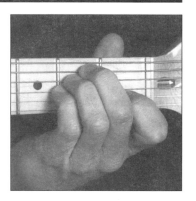

Gm7

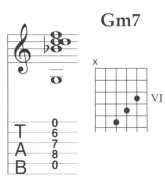

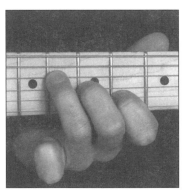

Bb

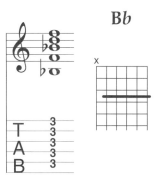

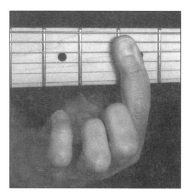

Gm7

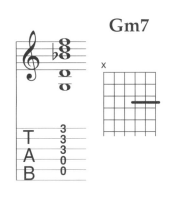

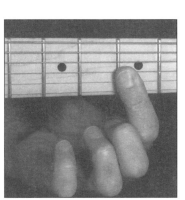

Bb6 add9

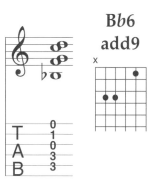

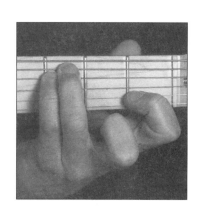

Gm11

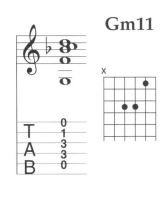

Bm

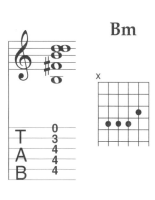

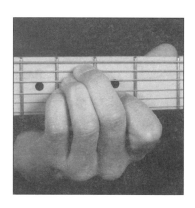

Am11

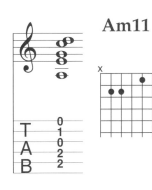

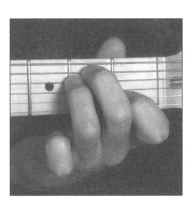

Bm7

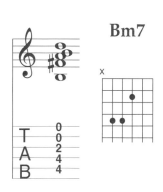

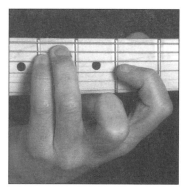

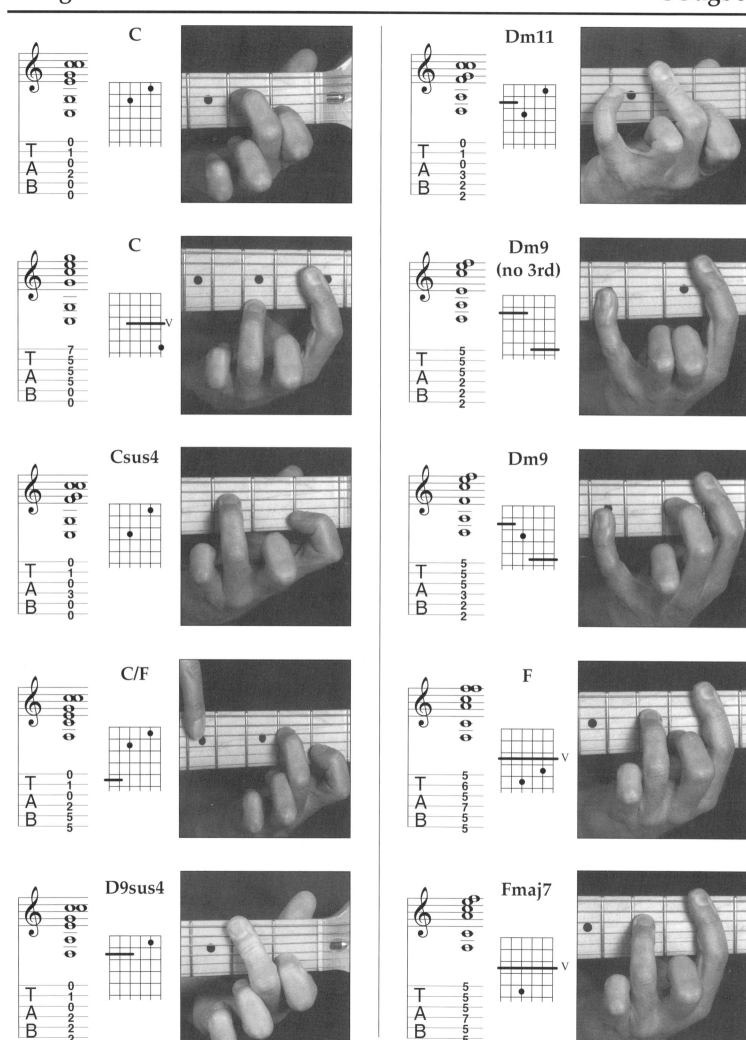

C

C

Csus4

C/F

D9sus4

Dm11

Dm9
(no 3rd)

Dm9

F

Fmaj7

Fmaj9

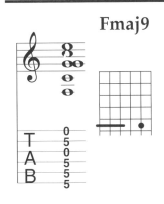 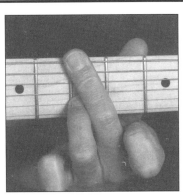 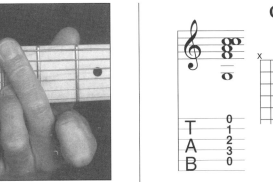

Eb6 add9

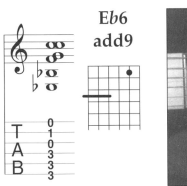 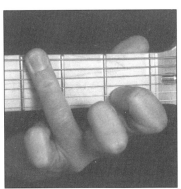 

Gadd9

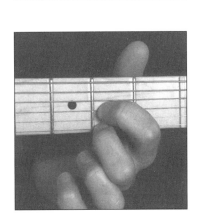

Gadd11

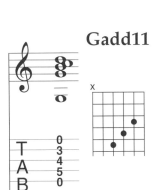 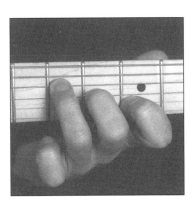

Gadd11

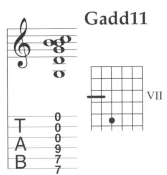 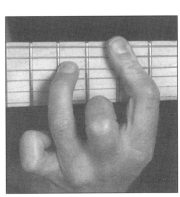

G11

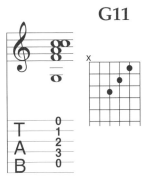 

Gmaj7 (#5)

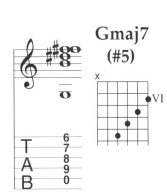 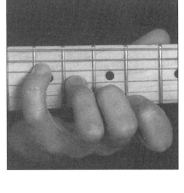

A/G

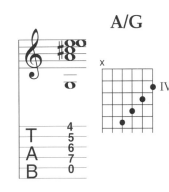 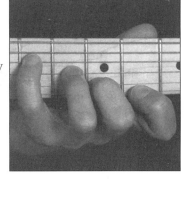

F#m11

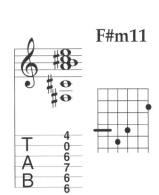 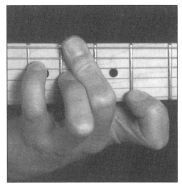

D/C

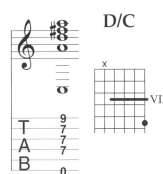 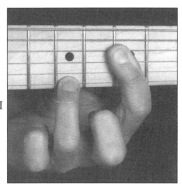

103

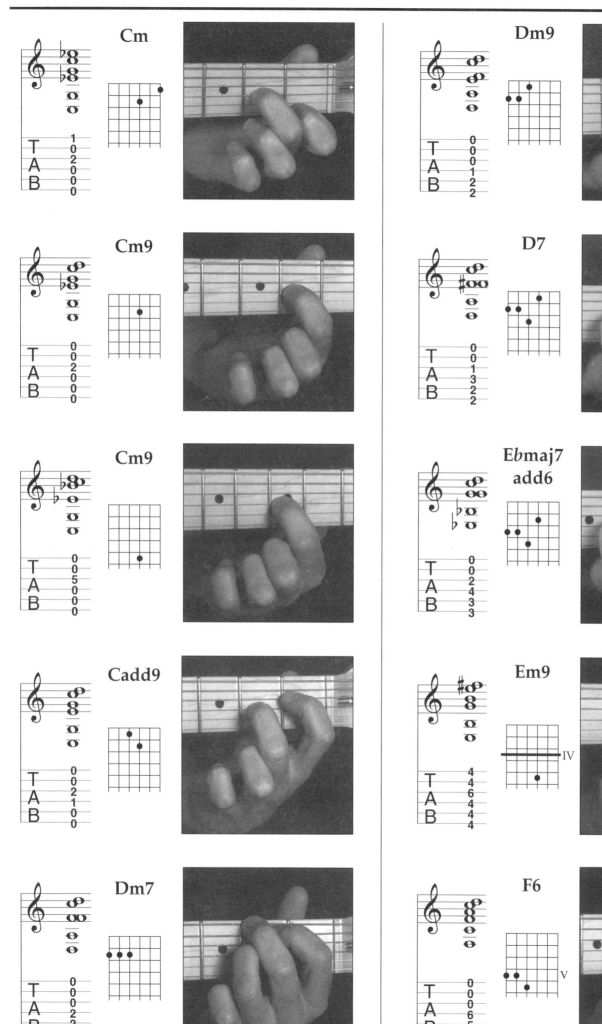
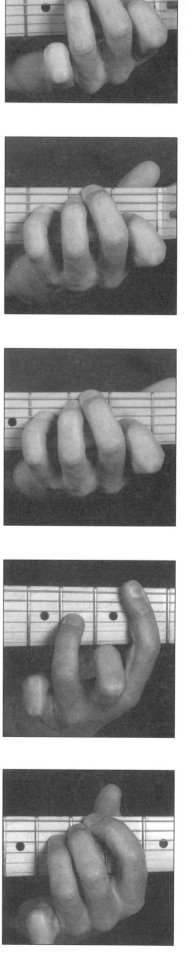

Cm

Cm9

Cm9

Cadd9

Dm7

Dm9

D7

E♭maj7
add6

Em9

F6

Fm6

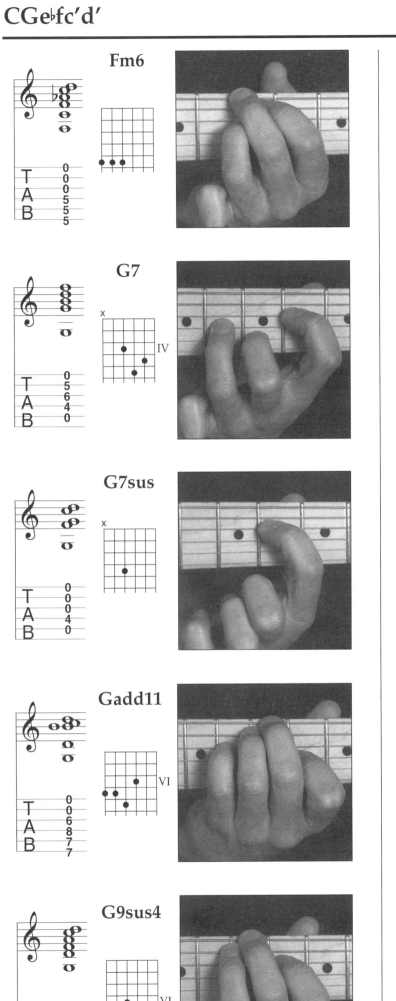

Gm9

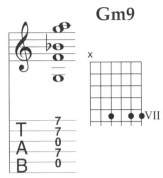
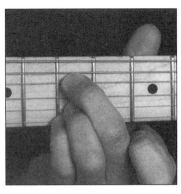

G7

Gm11

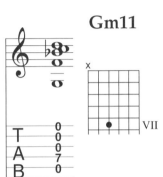
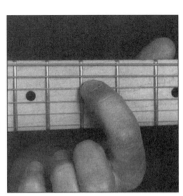

G7sus

Am11

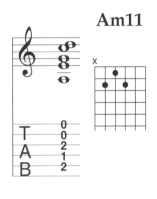
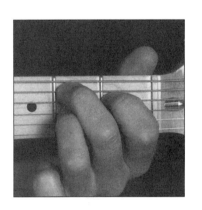

Gadd11

A11

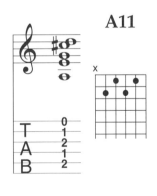

G9sus4

B♭add9

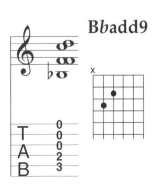
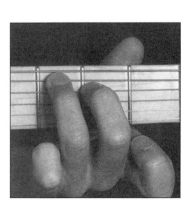

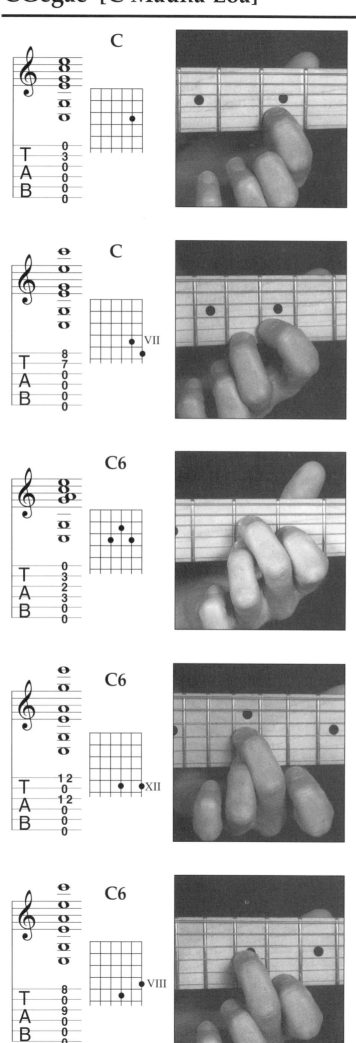

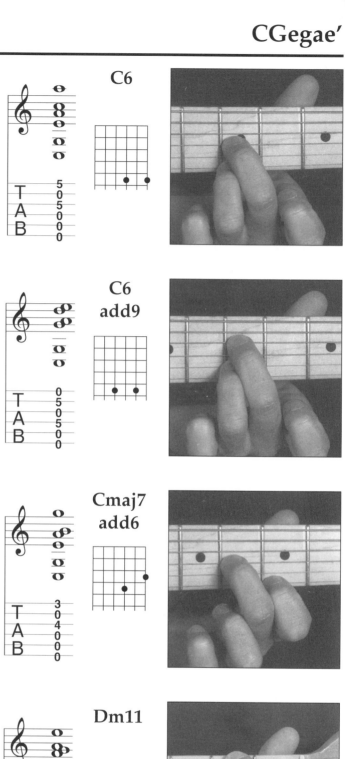

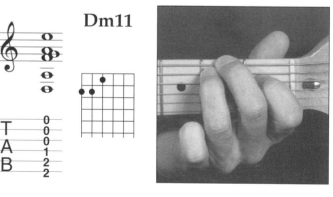

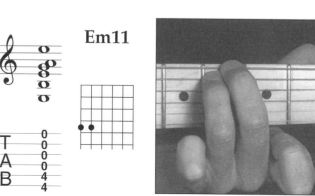

F6
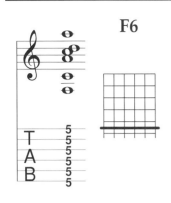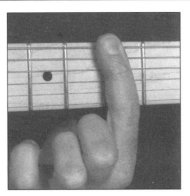

```
T  5
A  5
B  5
   5
   5
```

G13
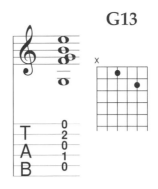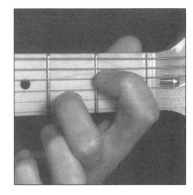

```
   0
   2
   1
   0
   0
```

Fmaj9
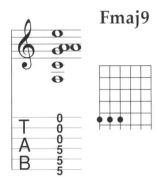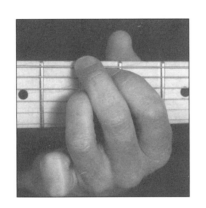

```
   0
   0
   0
   5
   5
   5
```

G13
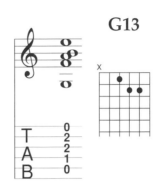

```
   0
   2
   2
   1
   0
```

G
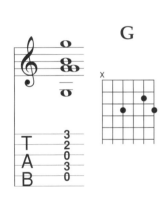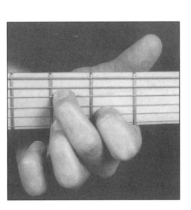

```
   3
   2
   0
   3
   0
```

G13sus4
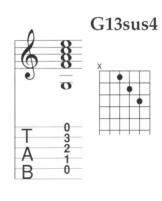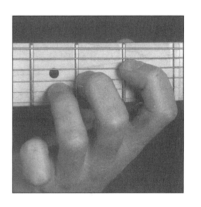

```
   0
   3
   2
   1
   0
```

G6
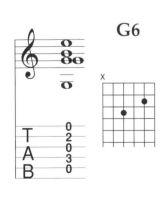

```
   0
   2
   0
   3
   0
```

Am7
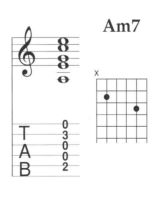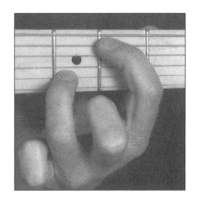

```
   0
   3
   0
   0
   2
```

Gadd9
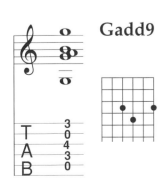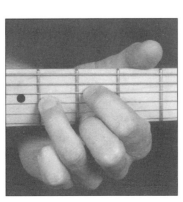

```
   3
   0
   4
   3
   0
```

A7
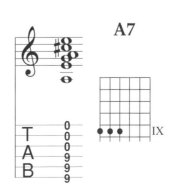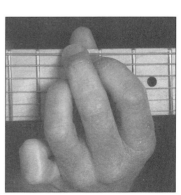

```
   0
   0
   0
   9
   9
   9
```
IX

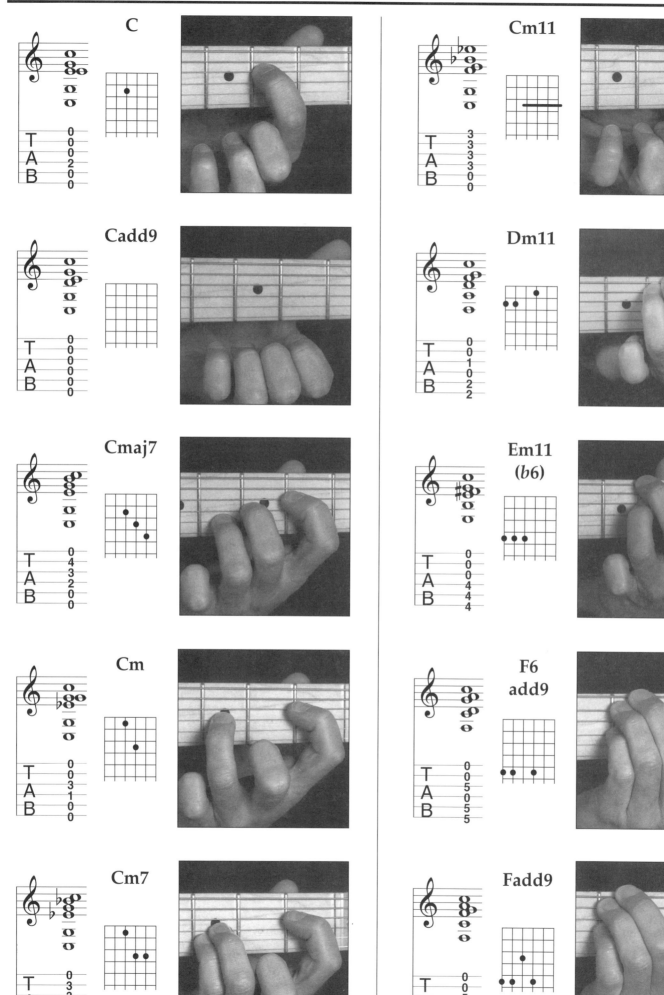

Fm9

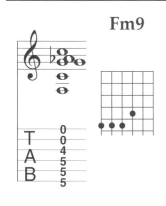
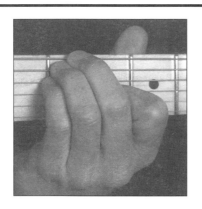

Gm7

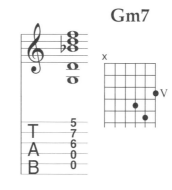
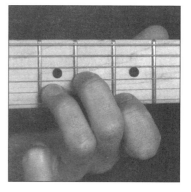

G

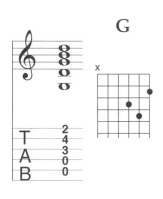
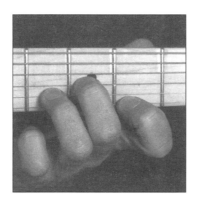

Gm11

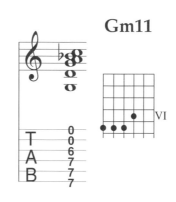
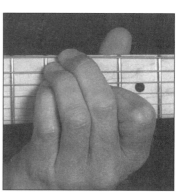

Gadd11

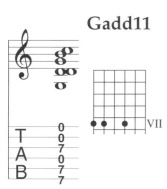
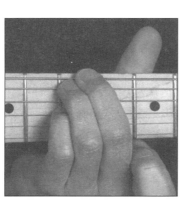

Am7

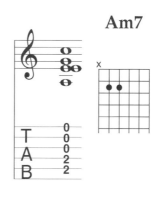
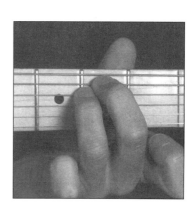

Gadd9

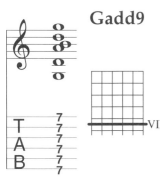
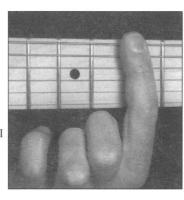

Am9

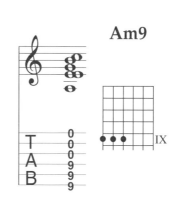
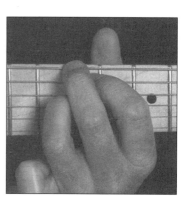

G9

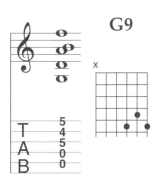
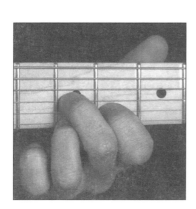

Bb6 add9

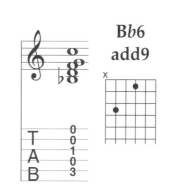
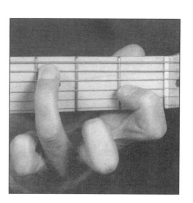

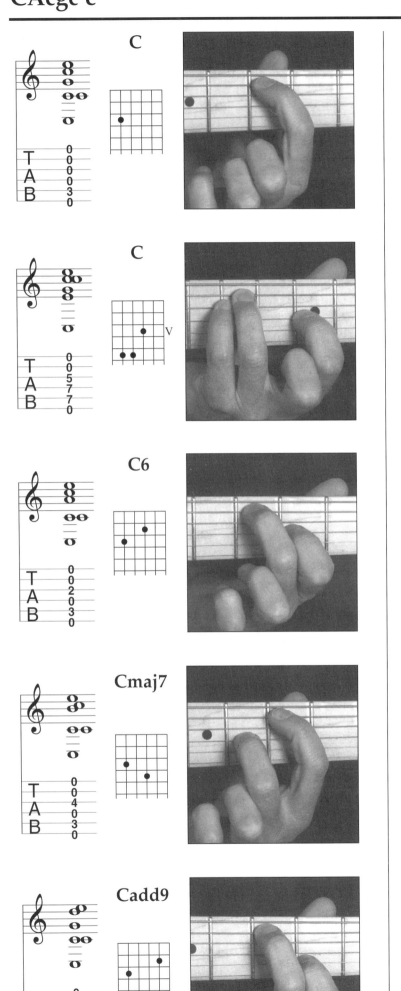
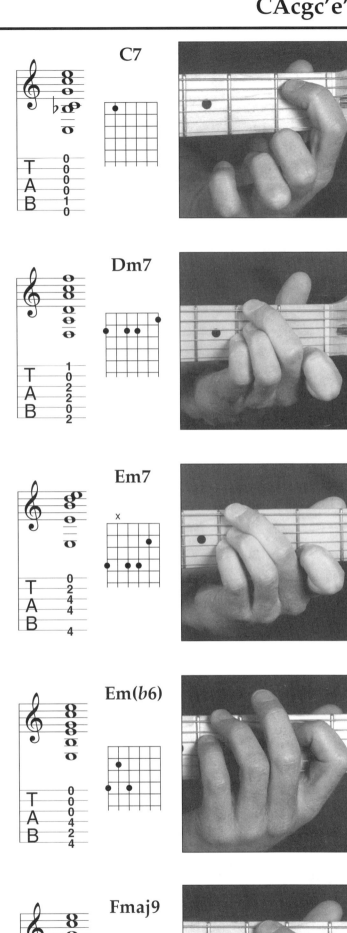

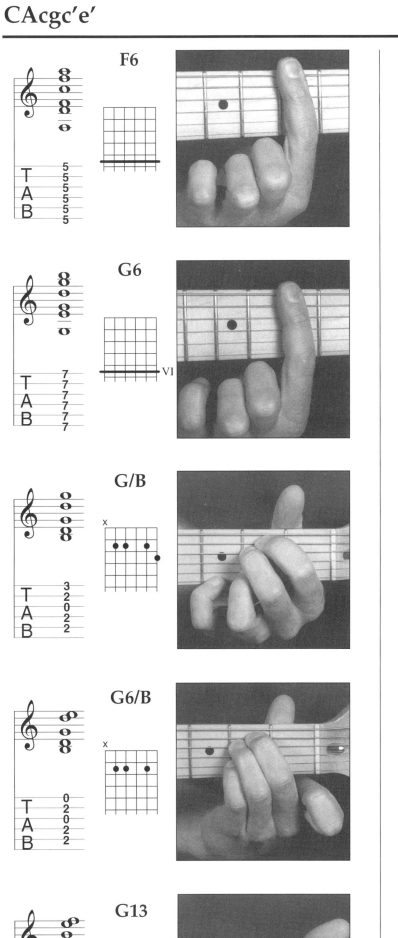

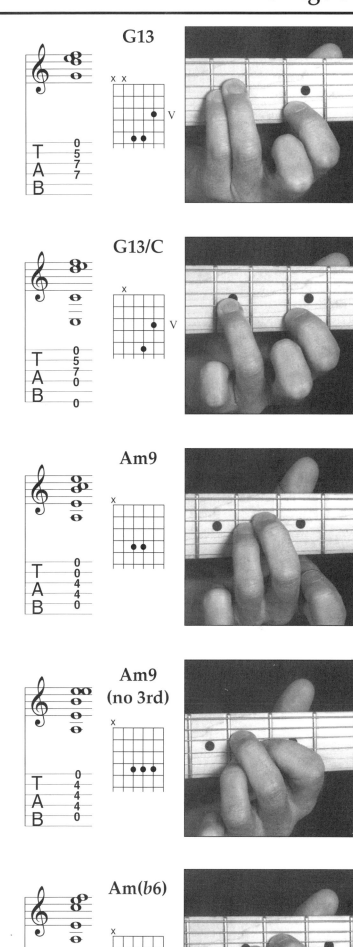

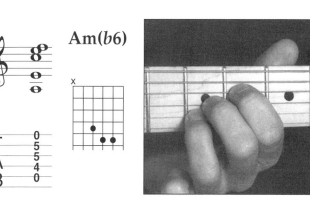

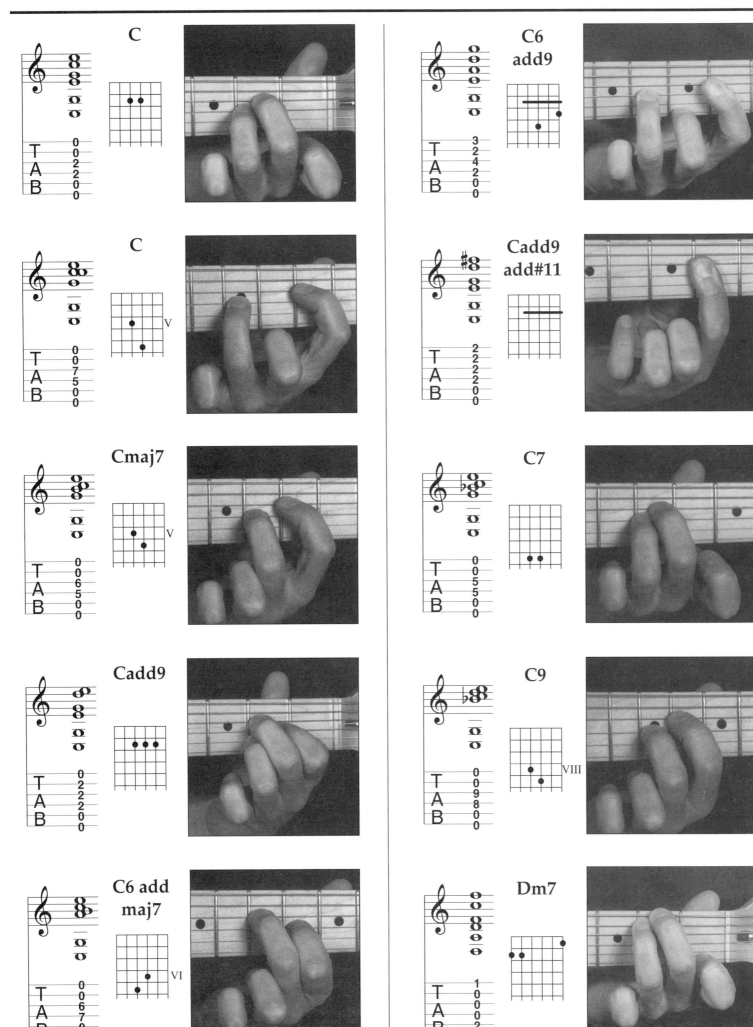

C

C

Cmaj7

Cadd9

C6 add maj7

C6 add9

Cadd9 add#11

C7

C9

Dm7

Dm9
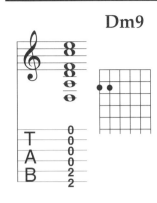
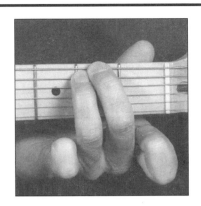

Eadd9
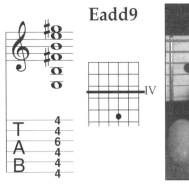
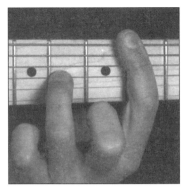

Dm11
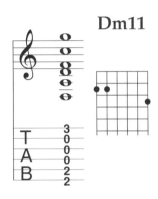

Fmaj9
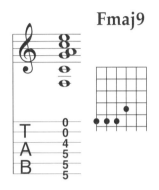
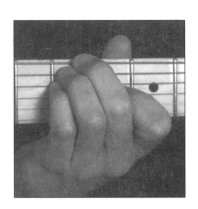

D
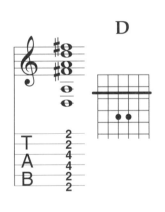
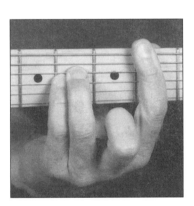

Fm9(#7)
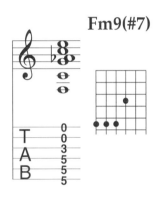
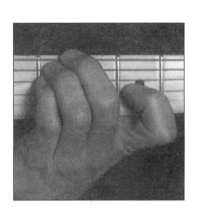

D9
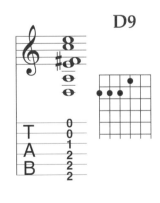
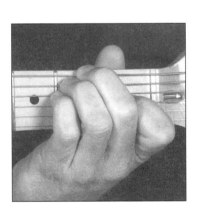

G
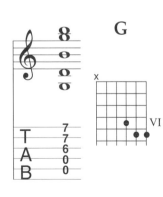

Em11
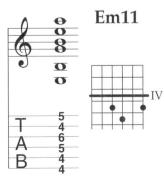
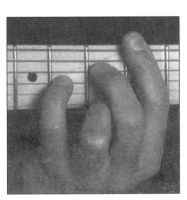

Gadd11
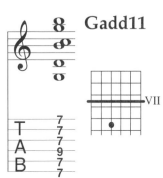
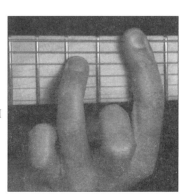

G6 add11

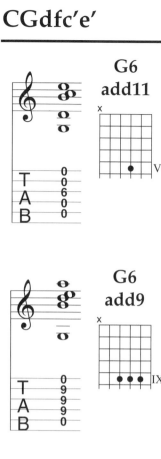

G6 add9

Gm6 add7

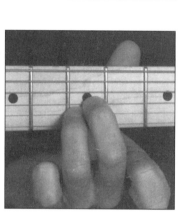

Gm6

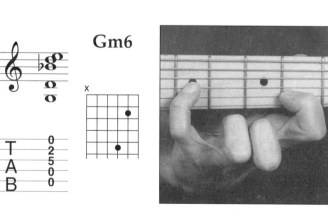

Gm11

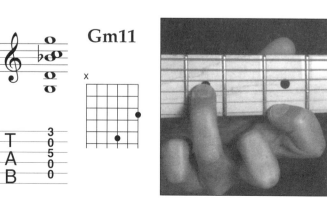

Am7

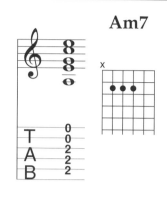
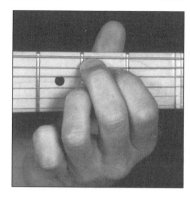

Am(b6)

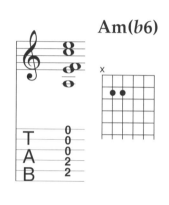
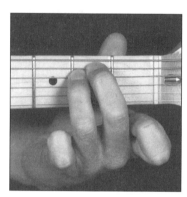

Am7/G

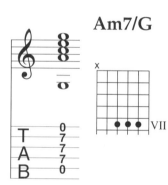
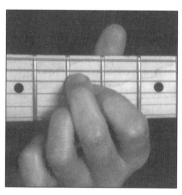

Bbadd9

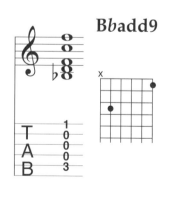
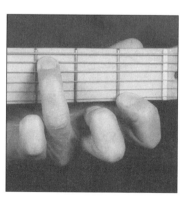

Bbadd9 add#11

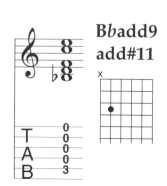
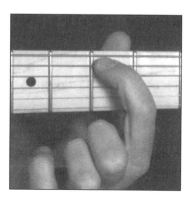

Martin D-28

Collings 12-Fret

EAdgc′f′ [All Fourths]   EAdgc′f′

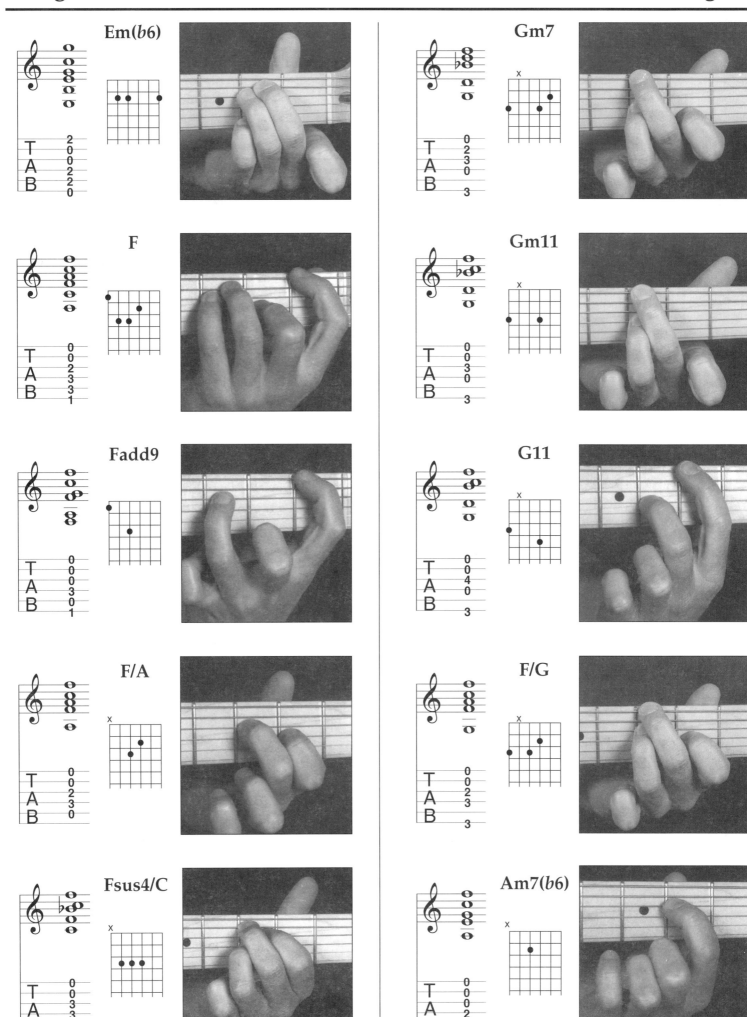

116

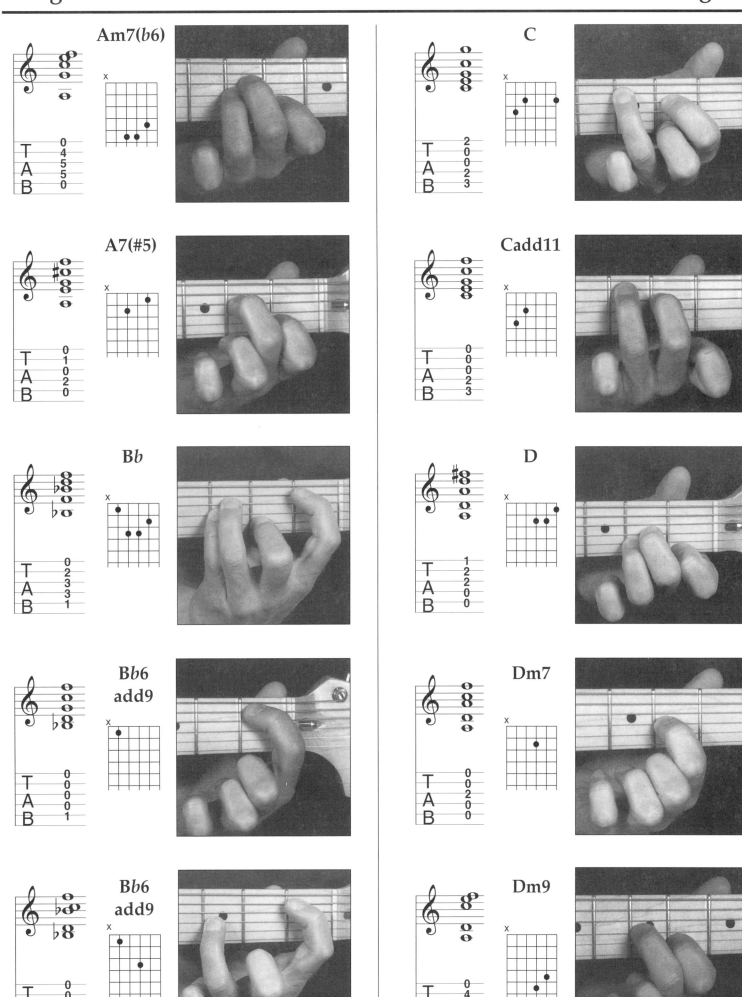

Am7(b6)

A7(#5)

Bb

Bb6
add9

Bb6
add9

C

Cadd11

D

Dm7

Dm9

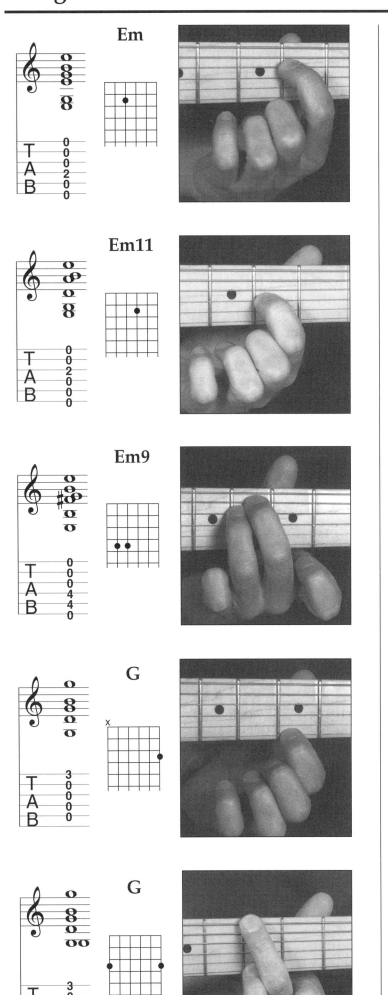

Em

Em11

Em9

G

G

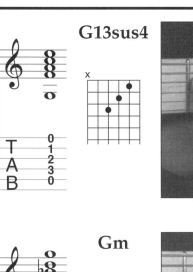

G13sus4

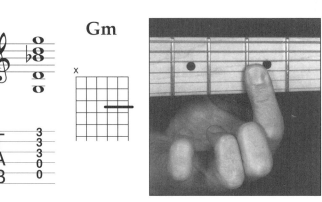

Gm

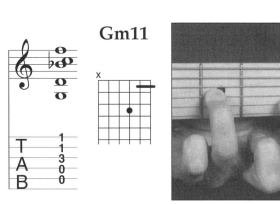

Gm11

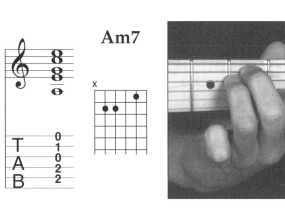

Am7

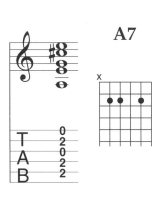

A7

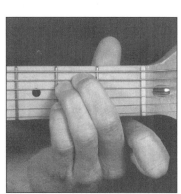

A/G

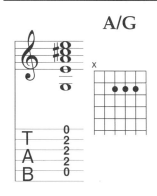

D/G

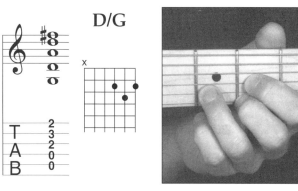

Bm11

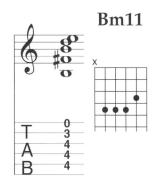
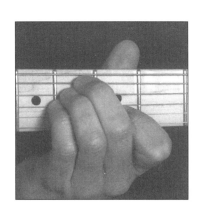

D6 add9/F#

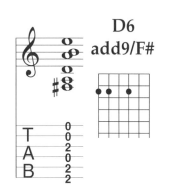
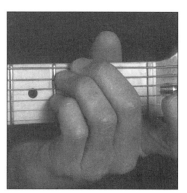

C

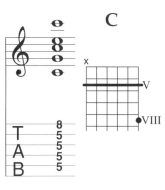
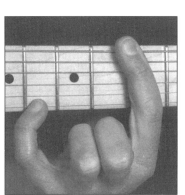

D9/F#

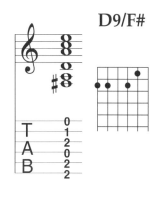
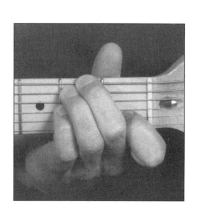

C/G

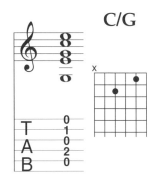
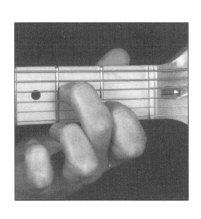

D7

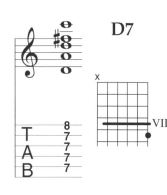
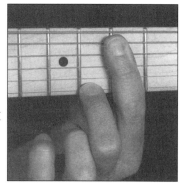

Cmaj7

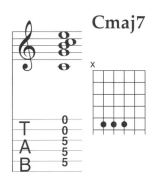
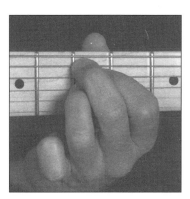

Dm9

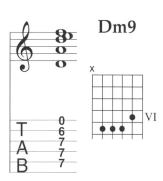
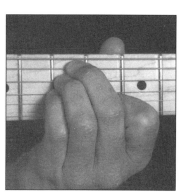

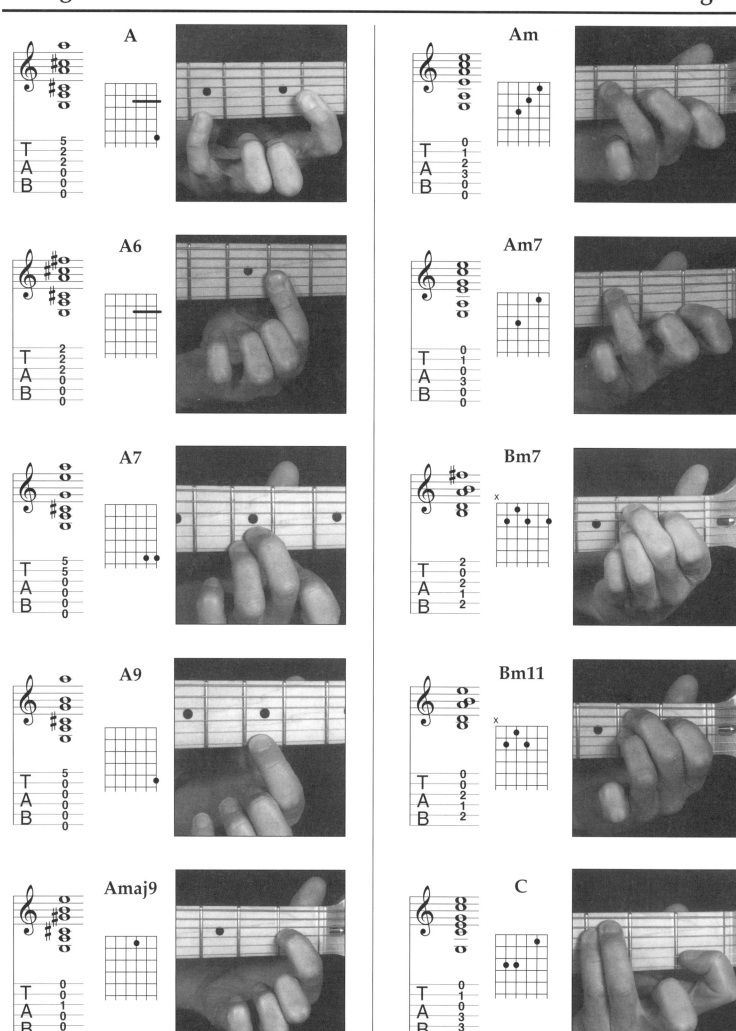

A

A6

A7

A9

Amaj9

Am

Am7

Bm7

Bm11

C

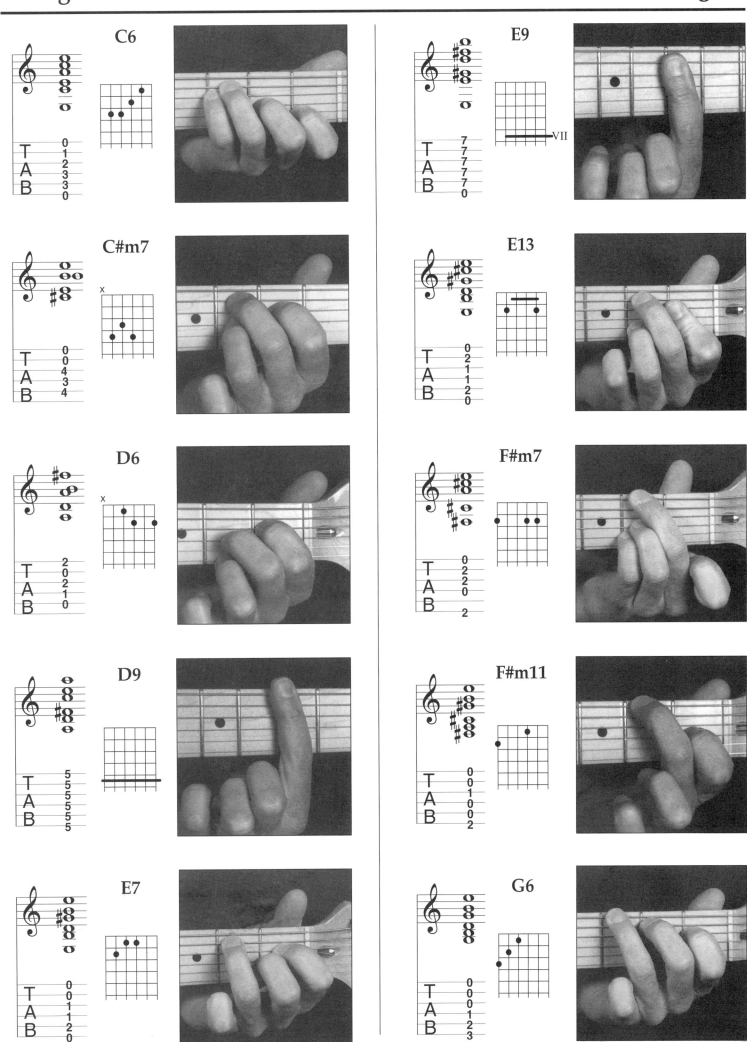

C6

C#m7

D6

D9

E7

E9

E13

F#m7

F#m11

G6

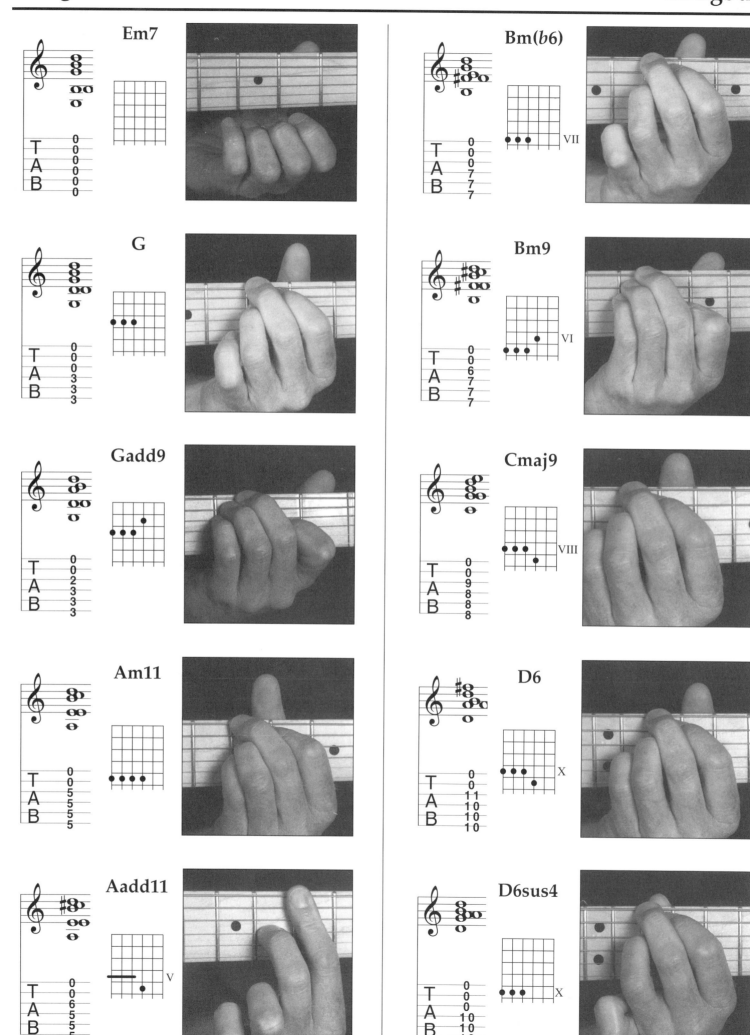

E5

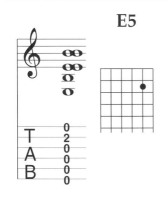
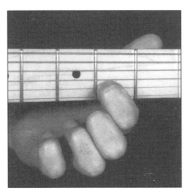

F#m11

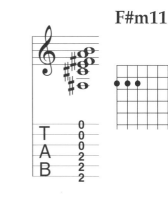
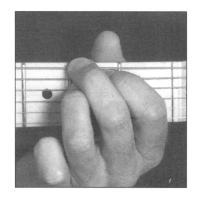

Em11

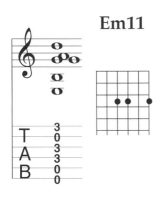
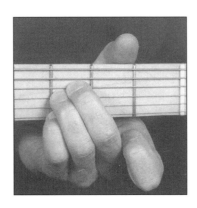

G6 add9

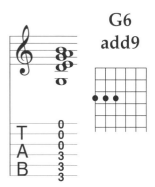
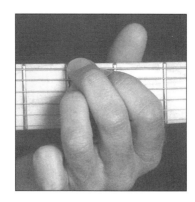

Em11

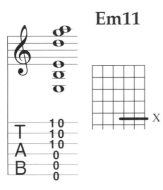
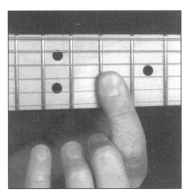

A5 add9

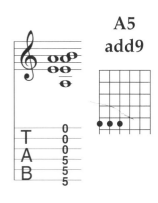
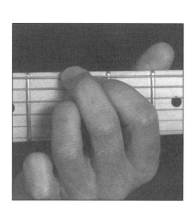

Eadd9 (no 3rd)

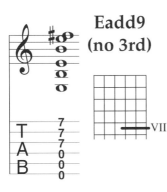
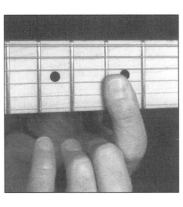

B7sus

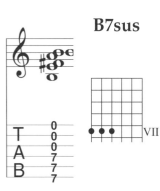
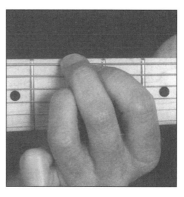

E

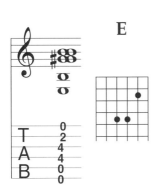
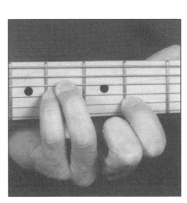

B7

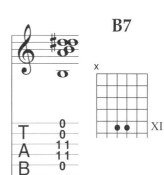
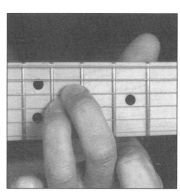

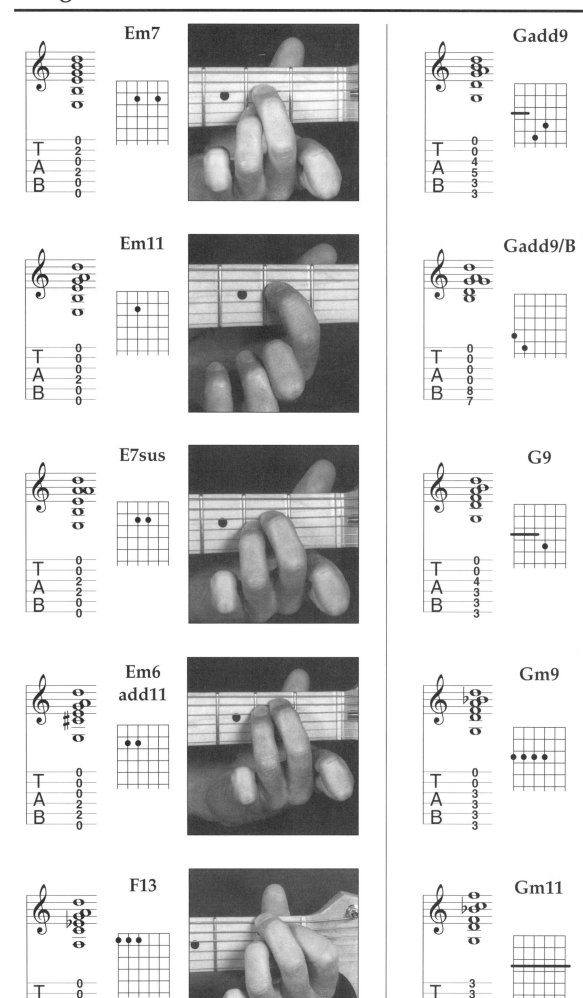

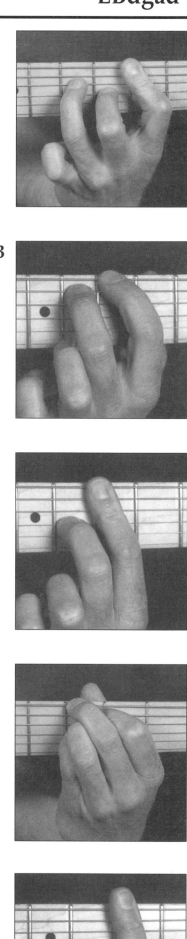

Em7

Em11

E7sus

Em6 add11

F13

Gadd9

Gadd9/B

G9

Gm9

Gm11

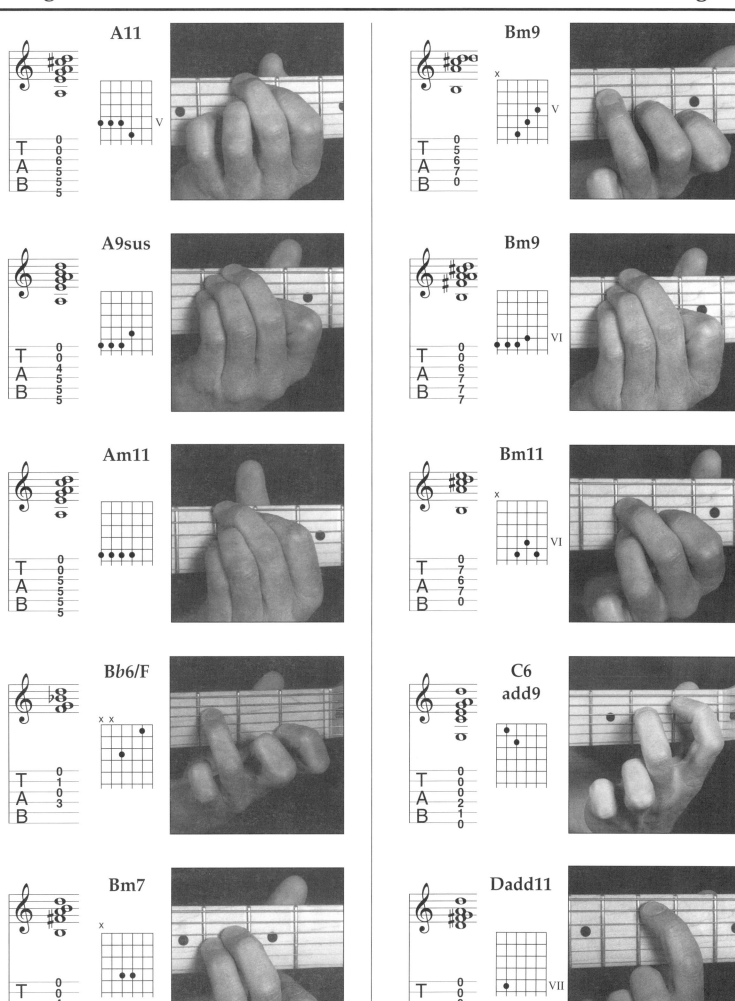

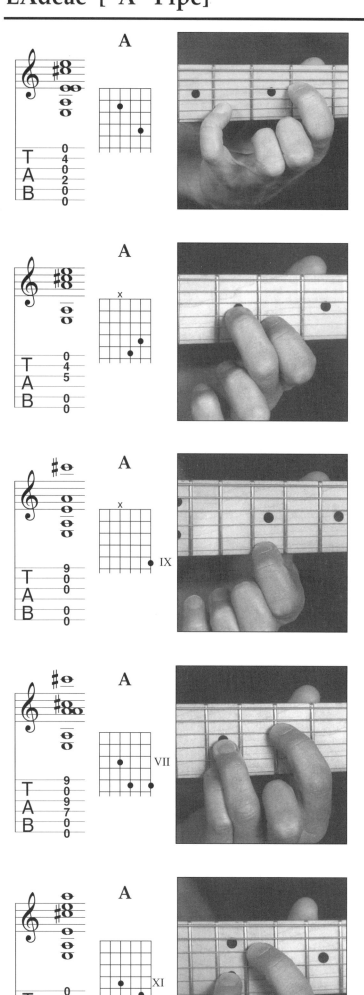

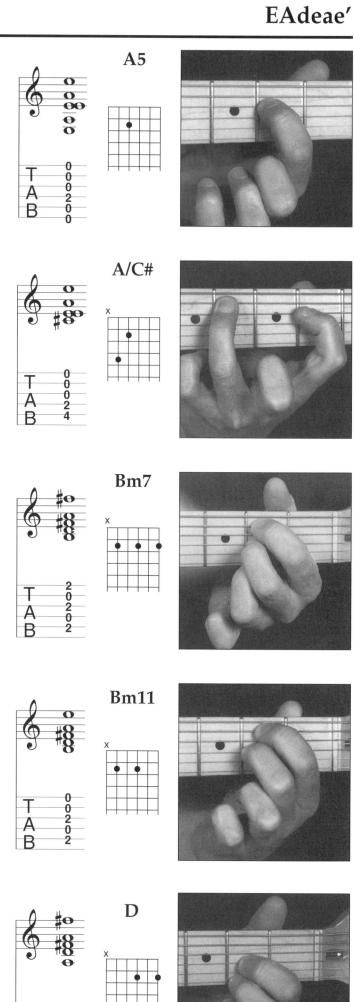

D
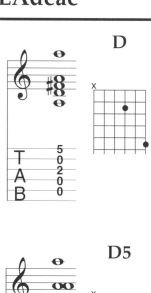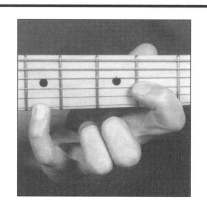

E5
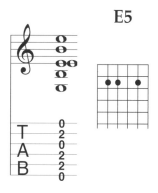

D5
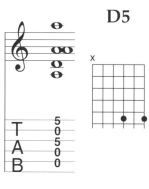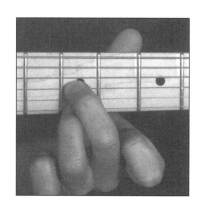

E7sus4
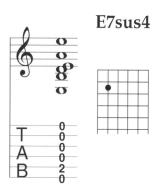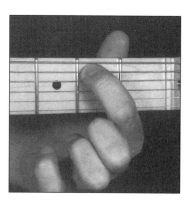

D/A
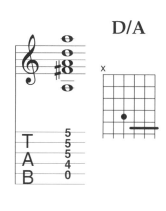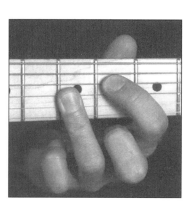

Em11
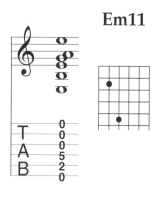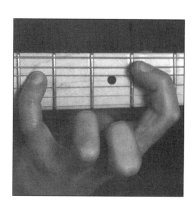

Dm
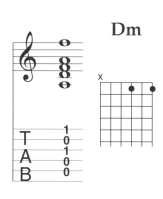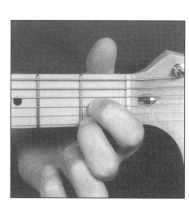

F#m7
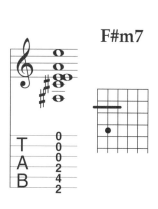

E
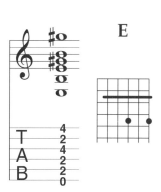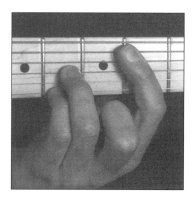

G6 add9
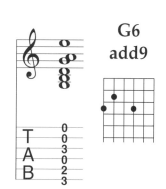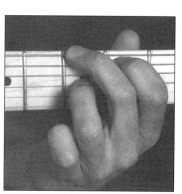

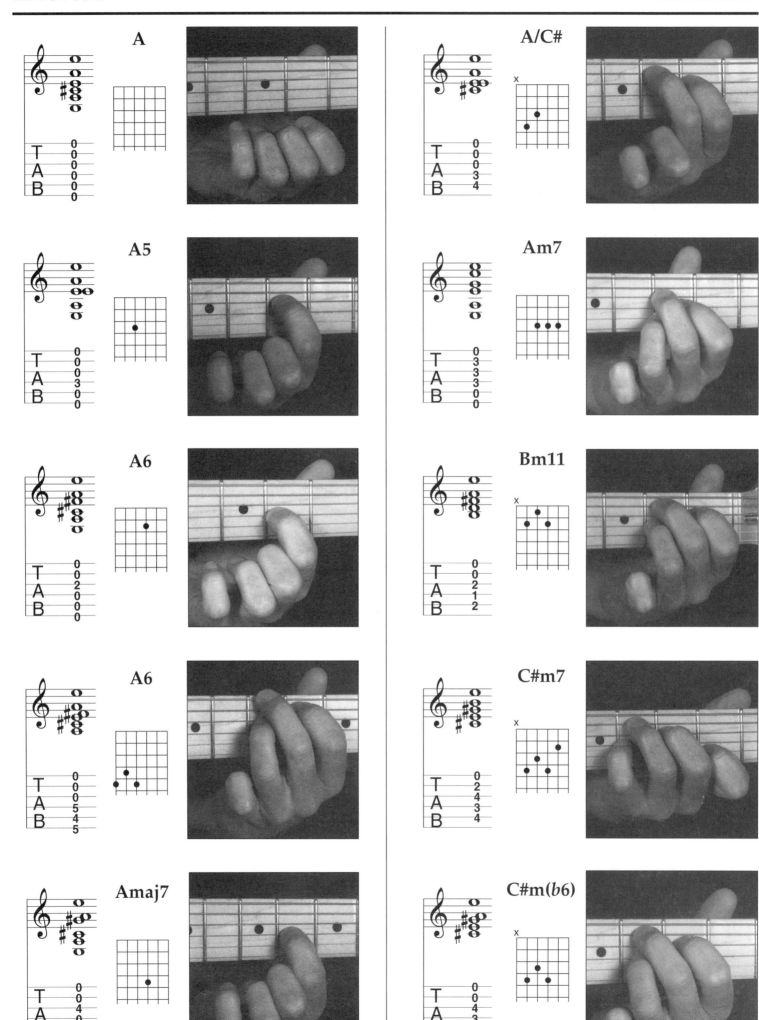

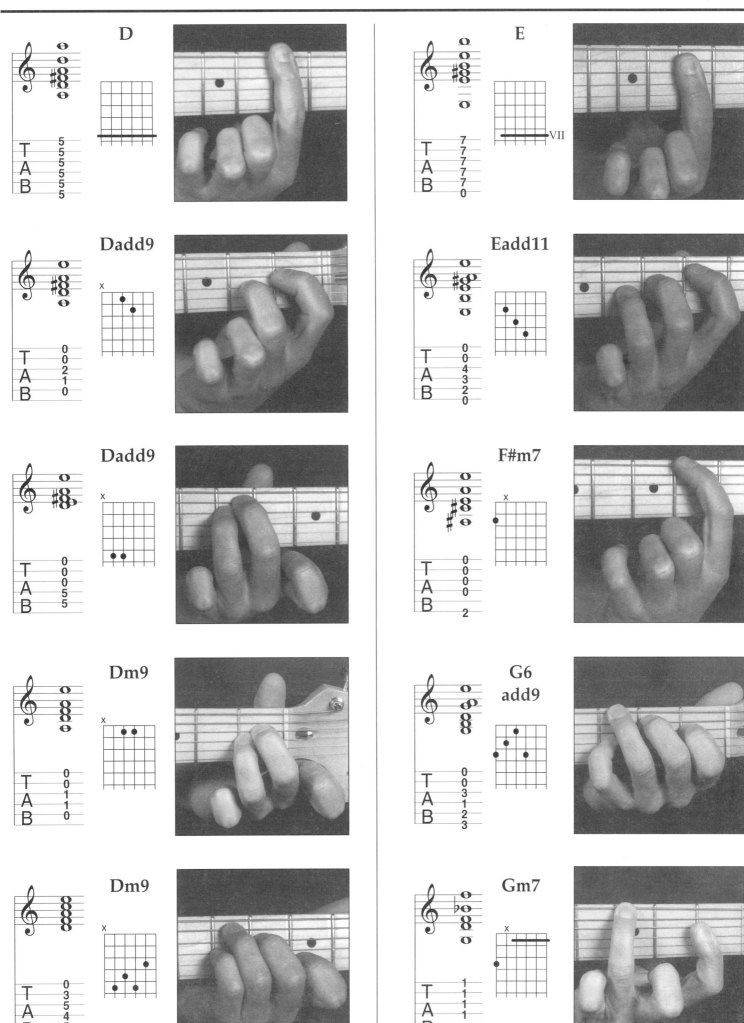

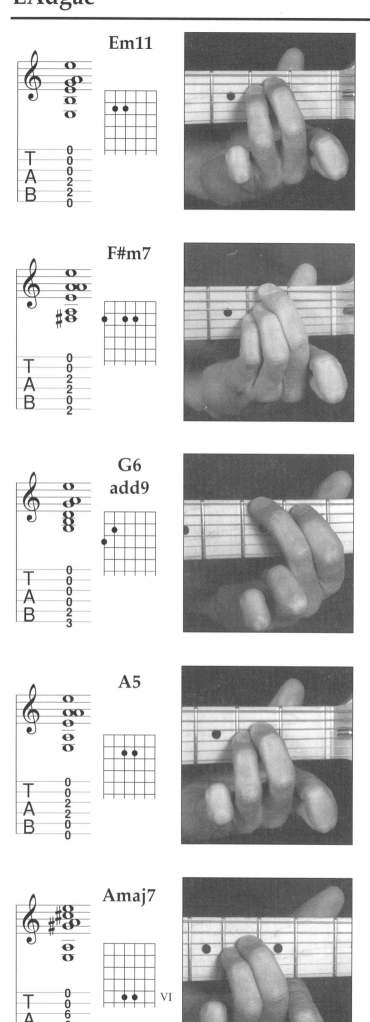

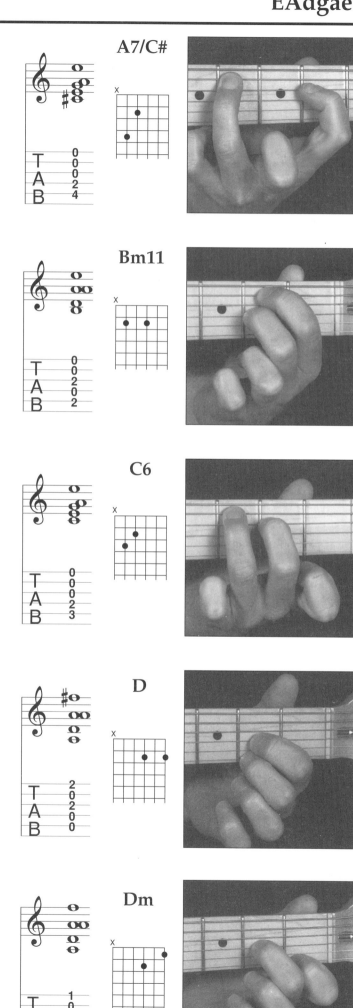

E
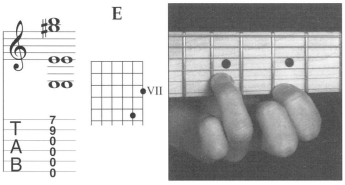

A7sus
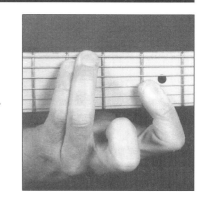

E
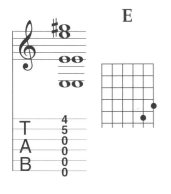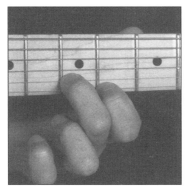

A/E
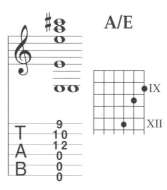

E7
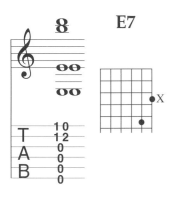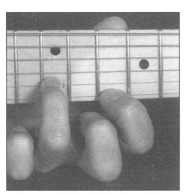

B5
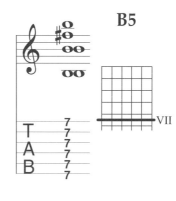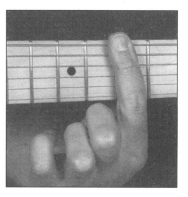

Em/G
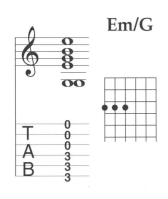

C#m/E
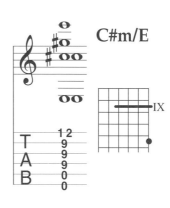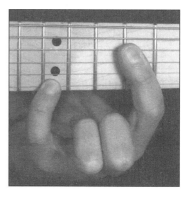

A5
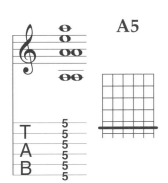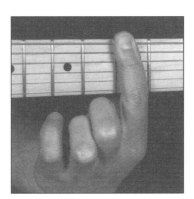

D/E
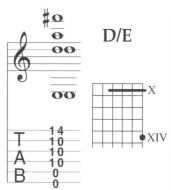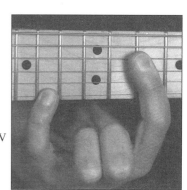

E5

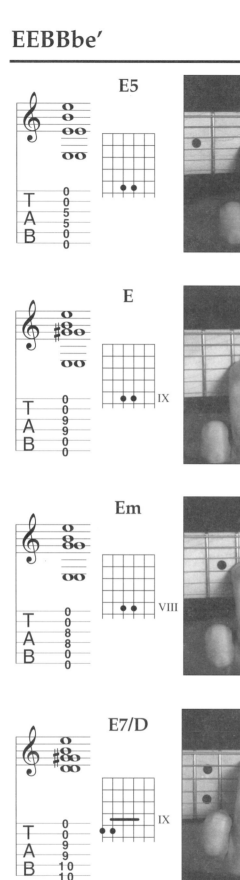

```
    0
    0
T   5
A   5
B   0
    0
```

E

```
    0
    0
T   9
A   9
B   0
    0
```

IX

Em

```
    0
    0
T   8
A   8
B   0
    0
```

VIII

E7/D

```
    0
    0
T   9
A   9
B   10
    10
```

IX

G6

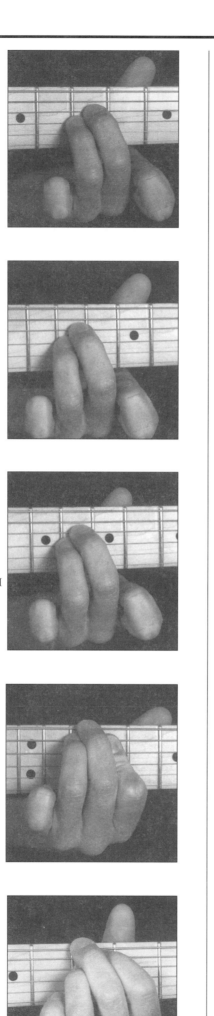

```
    0
    0
T   0
A   3
B   3
    3
```

Aadd9

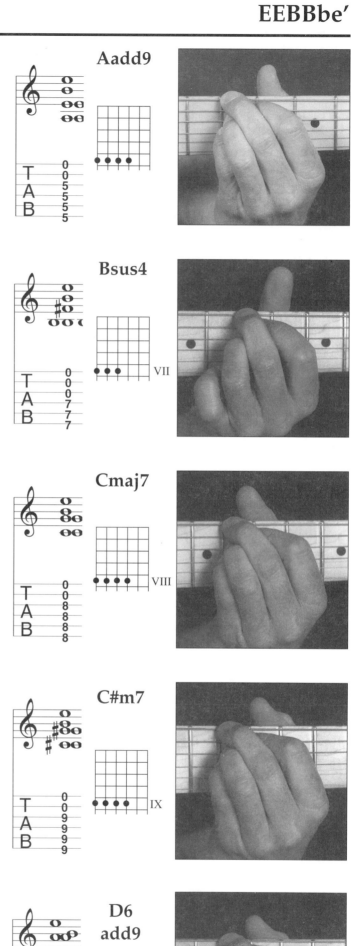

```
    0
    0
T   5
A   5
B   5
    5
```

Bsus4

```
    0
    0
T   0
A   7
B   7
    7
```

VII

Cmaj7

```
    0
    0
T   8
A   8
B   8
    8
```

VIII

C#m7

```
    0
    0
T   9
A   9
B   9
    9
```

IX

D6
add9

```
    0
    0
T   0
A   10
B   10
    10
    10
```

X

132

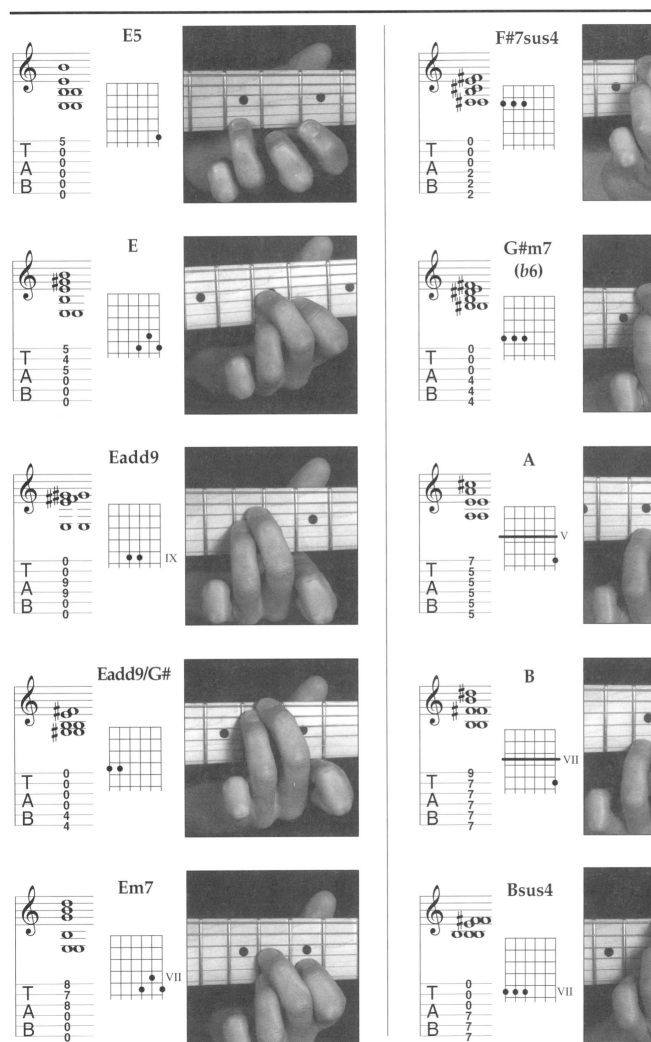

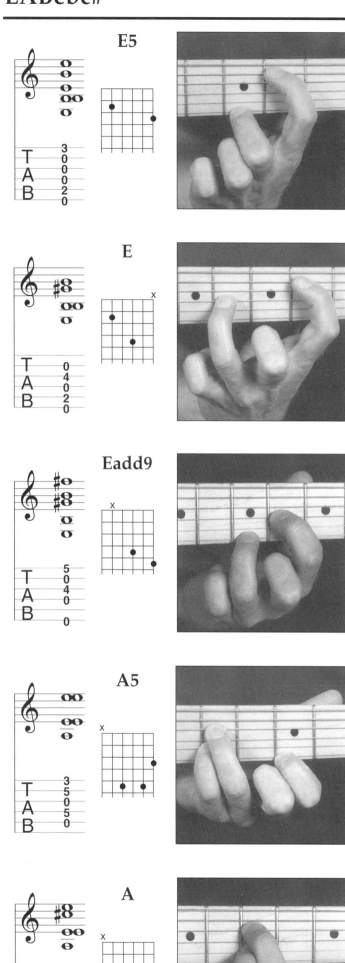

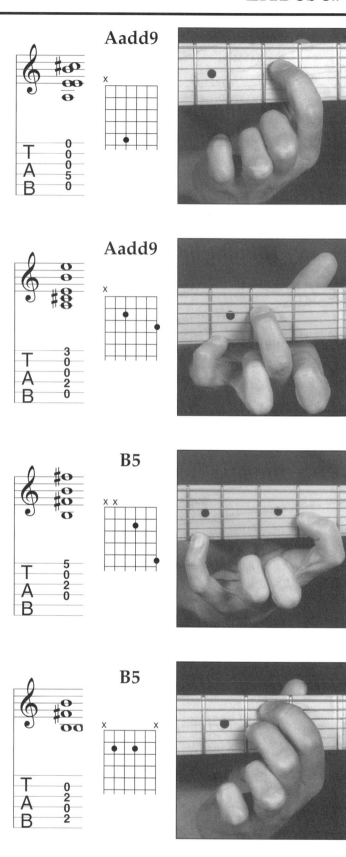

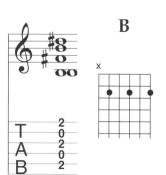

A

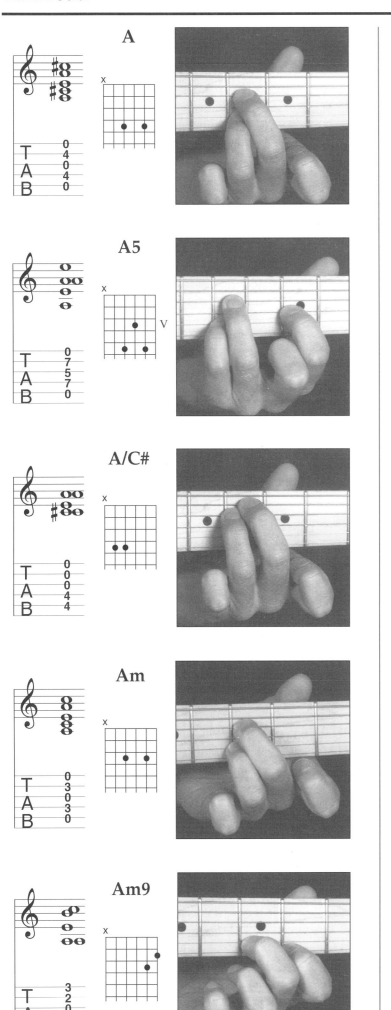

T A B
0
4
0
4
0

A5

0
7
5
7
0

A/C#

0
0
0
4
4

Am

0
3
0
3
0

Am9

3
2
0
0
0

E

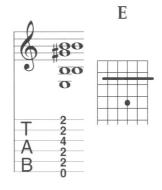

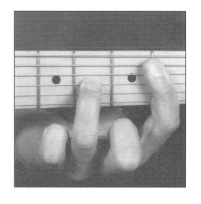

2
2
4
2
2
0

E5

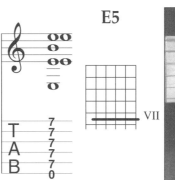

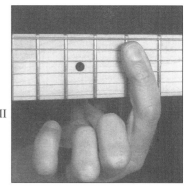

VII

7
7
7
7
7
0

Eadd11

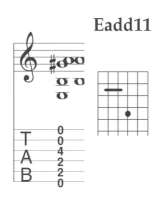

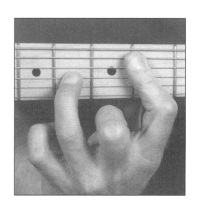

0
0
4
2
2
0

Em11

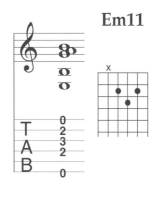

0
2
3
2
0

F/A

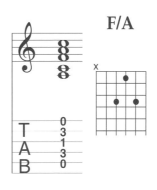

0
3
1
3
0

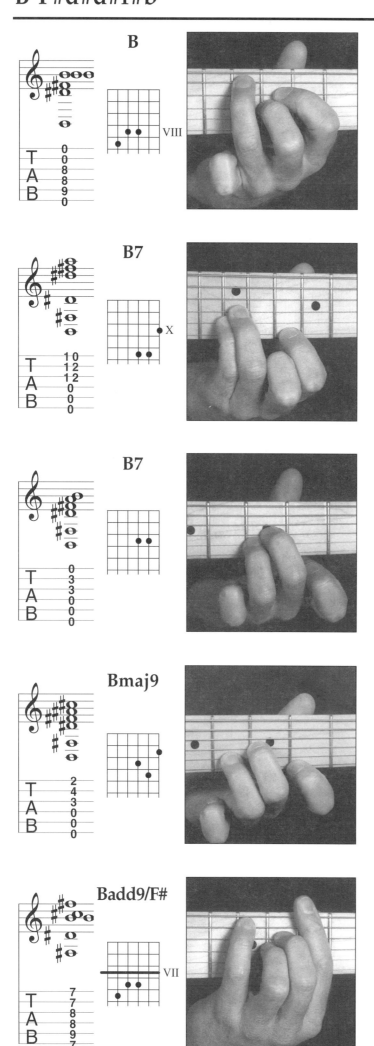

B

B7

B7

Bmaj9

Badd9/F#

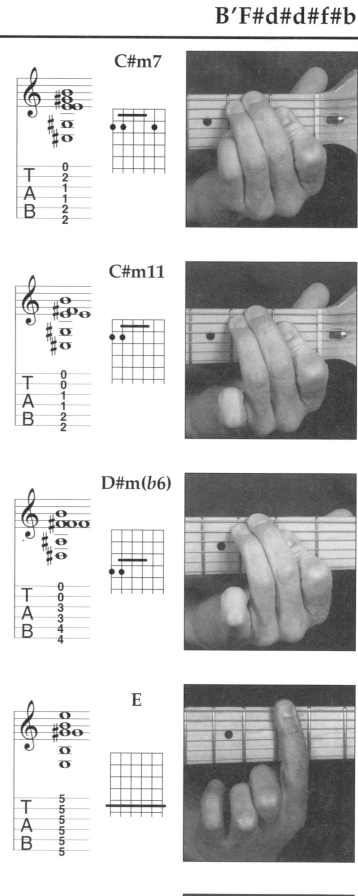

C#m7

C#m11

D#m(b6)

E

Eadd9

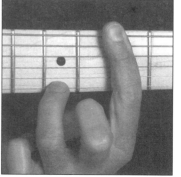

Em9

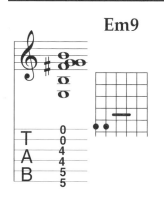
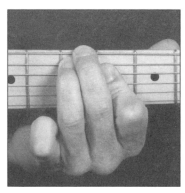

```
T    0
A    4
B    4
     5
     5
```

F#m11

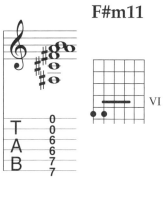
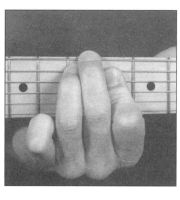

VI

```
T    0
A    0
B    6
     6
     7
     7
```

Em/G

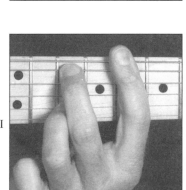
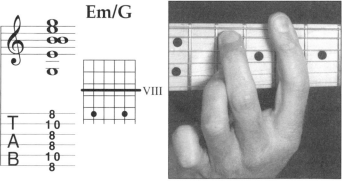

VIII

```
T    8
A    10
B    8
     8
     10
     8
```

G#m7

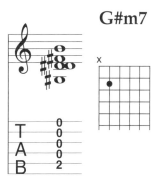

x

```
T    0
A    0
B    0
     0
     2
     2
```

F#

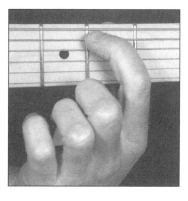

VII

```
T    7
A    7
B    7
     7
     7
     7
```

G#m7

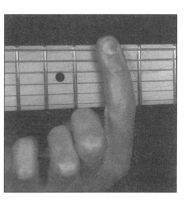

IX

```
T    0
A    0
B    0
     0
     0
     9
     9
```

F#

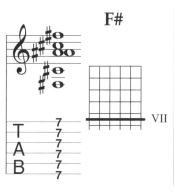
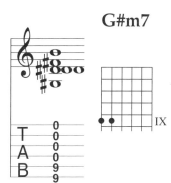

x

```
T    2
A    4
B    3
     3
     0
```

G#m9

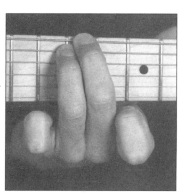

x

```
T    0
A    4
B    3
     0
     2
```

F#7

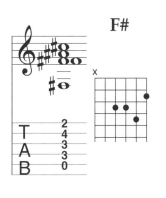
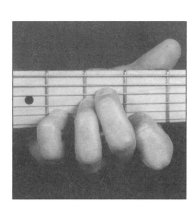

VII

```
T    7
A    10
B    7
     7
     7
     7
```

Aadd9/E

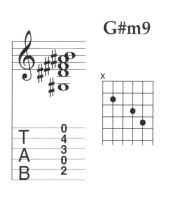

V

```
T    5
A    5
B    6
     6
     7
     5
```

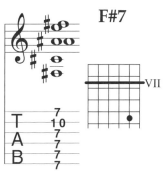
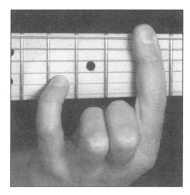
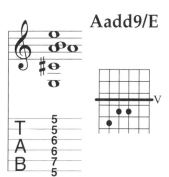
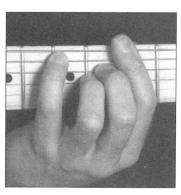

137

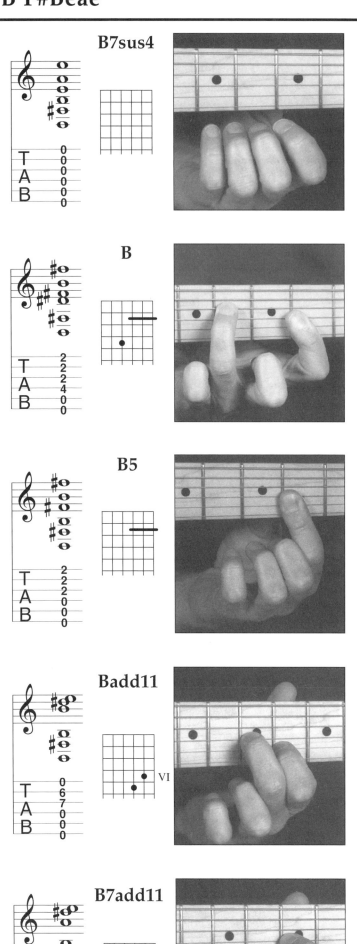

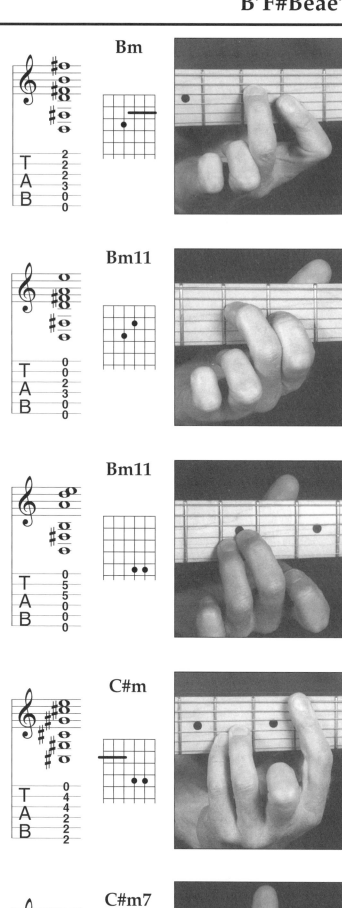

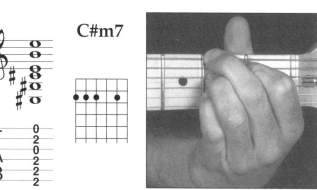

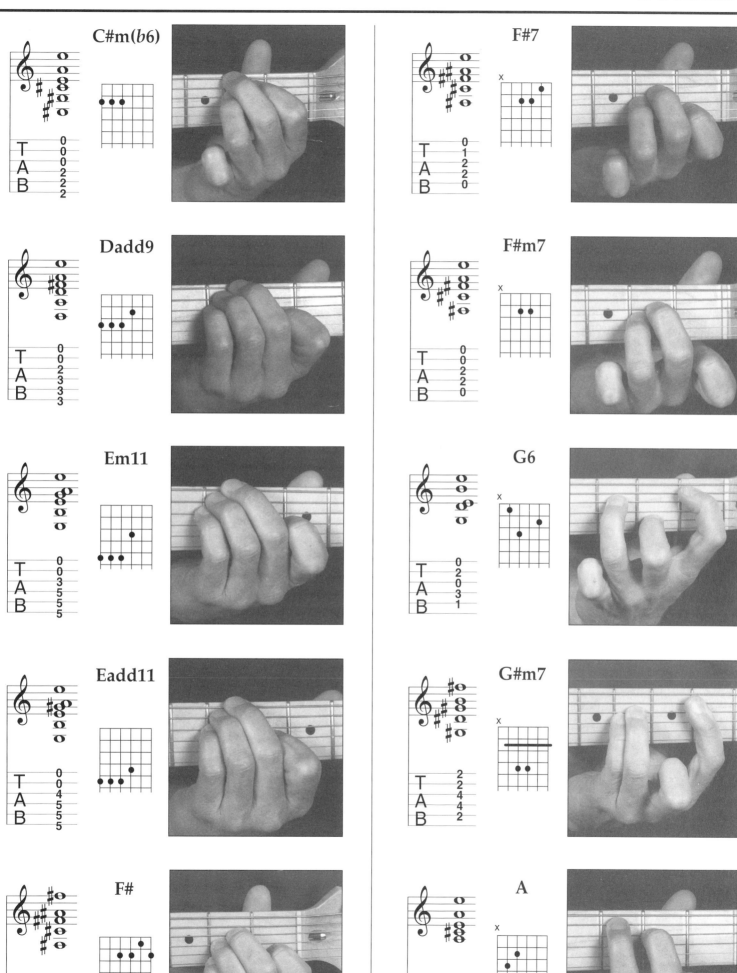

C#m(b6)

F#7

Dadd9

F#m7

Em11

G6

Eadd11

G#m7

F#

A

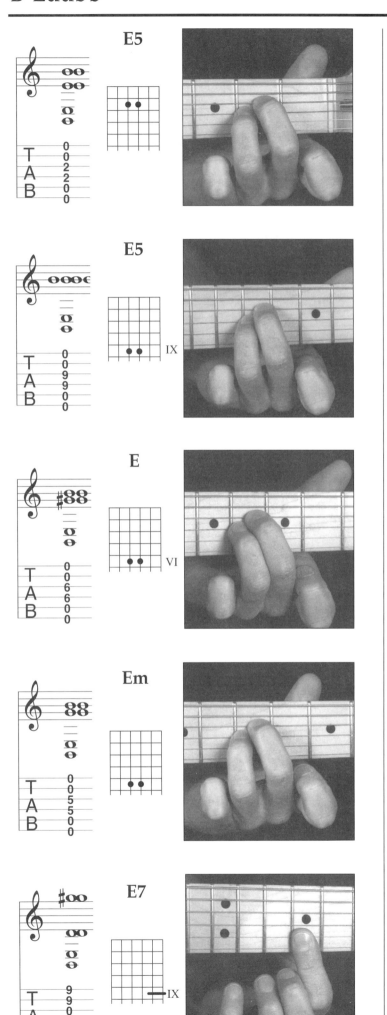

E5

E5

E

Em

E7

Em7

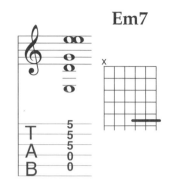

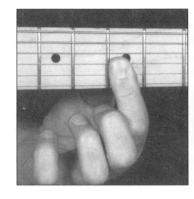

F#m

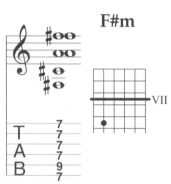

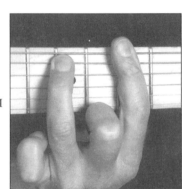

G

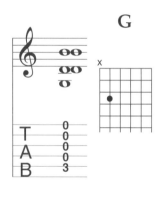

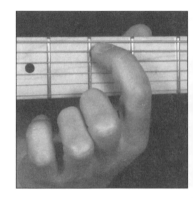

Bm

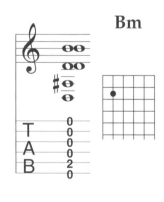

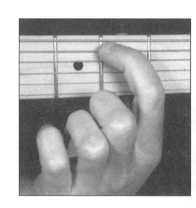

Bm7

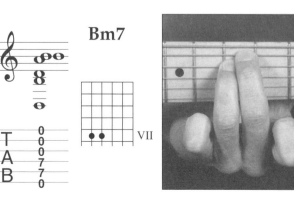

G5

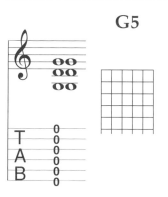

Gadd9 (no 3rd)

G(unison)

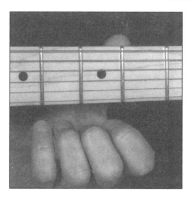

Bb6

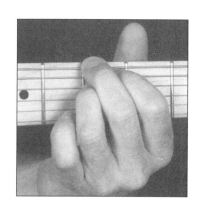

G

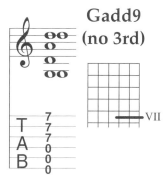

Bm(b6)

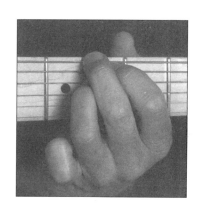

Gm

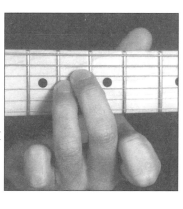

C5

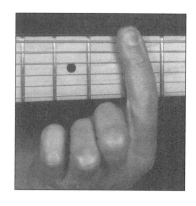

Gm7

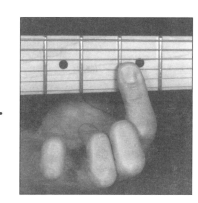

D5

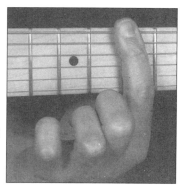

Artist Listings

Tunings   Sampling of Artists Who Use Each Tuning

Page		
D-Bass Tunings		
6	D A d g b e′	James Taylor, Ry Cooder, Leo Kottke, Pete Seeger, Richard Thompson
14	D A d g b d′	Neil Young, Stephen Stills, Adrian Legg, Ed Gerhard, Mark Hanson
19	D A d g b b	Sound Garden ("Face Pollution")
20	D A d g a d′	Pierre Bensusan, Michael Hedges, Doyle Dykes, Bert Jansch, Jimmy Page, Alex deGrassi, Peppino D'Agostino, Nanci Griffith, Phil Keaggy
26	D A d g b♭ e′	John Renbourn ("Palermo Snow")
28	D A e g a d′	Joni Mitchell ("Cool Water", "Slouching Toward Bethlehem")
30	D A d f# b e′	Lutenists
32	D A d f# a d′	John Lee Hooker, Joni Mitchell, Allman Brothers, Dougie MacLean, Leo Kottke, David Wilcox, John Hammond, George Thorogood
37	D A d f a d′	Skip James, Bukka White, Peter Finger, Martin Simpson
40	D A d f# a c#′	Hawaiian Slack Key artists
42	D A d e a d′	Michael Hedges, Alex deGrassi, Pat Kirtley, Bill Mize
46	D A d d a d′	David Crosby
47	D A d d g c′	David Crosby
48	D A d g a f#′	Nick Drake ("Place to Be")
50	D A c g c′ e′	Michael Hedges ("Layover")
52	D A c# e a e′	Mary Chapin Carpenter ("I Am a Town")
53	D G d g b d′	Eric Clapton, Robert Johnson, Rory Block, Jorma Kaukonen
58	D G d f# b d′	Ray Kane′ ("Punahele"), Mark Hanson ("Angels We Have Heard...")
60	D G d g c′ d′	Martin Simpson, Steve Baughmann, Eric Schoenberg
64	D G d g b♭ d′	John Fahey, Laurence Juber, John Renbourn, Peter Finger
68	D G d g a d′	Nancy Griffith, Dave Evans, Dick Gaughan
71	D G d g b e′	Chet Atkins, Muriel Anderson, Duck Baker, Adrian Legg
74	D G c d a d′	Nick Drake ("Road")
C-Bass Tunings		
76	C G d g b e′	Fleetwood Mac ("Never Going Back Again"), Hawaiian Slack Key
79	C G c g c′ e′	Leo Kottke, Peter Lang, Tom Rush, Bruce Cockburn
82	C G c g c′ e♭′	Al Petteway, Laurence Juber, Martin Simpson, Michael Coulon
86	C G c g c′ d′	Martin Simpson ("Granuaile", "Bob's Song")
88	C G c f c′ d′	Martin Simpson ("Young Man")
90	C G c f c′ e′	Nick Drake ("Hanging On A Star")
92	C G c g a d′	Keola Beamer ("Eku'u Morning Dew"), Hawaiian Slack Key
94	C G d g a d′	El McMeen ("Carolan's Dream")
98	C G d g b d′	Joni Mitchell ("Cold Blue Steel and Sweet Fire")
102	C G d g b c′	Michael Hedges ("Rickover's Dream")
104	C G e♭ f c′ d′	David Wilcox ("Please Don't Call")
106	C G e g a e′	"C Mauna Loa," Hawaiian Slack Key
108	C G d e g c′	Joni Mitchell ("Night Ride Home")
110	C A c g c′ e′	Led Zeppelin ("Bron-Y-Aur")
112	C G d f c′ e′	Joni Mitchell ("Just Like This Train")
E-Bass Tunings		
116	E A d g c′ f′	William Ackerman ("Bricklayer's Beautiful Daughter"), jazz players
118	E G d g b e′	Duck Baker ("Fanteladdo")
120	E A c# g b e′	Chet Atkins, John Knowles
122	E B B g b d	Ani Di Franco ("Cradle and All"), Smashing Pumpkins
123	E B e e a b	Sonic Youth ("Eric's Trip", Kissability)
124	E B d g a d′	David Crosby ("Guinnevere")
126	E A d e a e′	Martin Carthy, John Renbourn
128	E A c# e a e′	Chris Proctor, Pearl Jam
130	E A d g a e′	Mary Chapin Carpenter ("Something of a Dreamer"), John Renbourn, Ed Gerhard ("Crow")
131	E E e e b e′	Stephen Stills ("Suite: Judy Blue Eyes")
132	E E B B b e′	Soundgarden ("Somewhere")
133	E E B B e′ f#′	Sonic Youth ("Chapel Hill")
134	E A B e b c#′	Steve Baughmann ("Bony Crossing the Alps")
135	E A A e a a	Steve Baughmann ("Iberian Gathering")
B-Bass Tunings		
136	B′ F# d# d# f# b	Joni Mitchell ("Turbulent Indigo", "How Do You Stop")
138	B′ F# B e a e′	Joni Mitchell ("Magdalene Laudries")
140	B′ E d d b b	Sonic Youth ("Skink")
G-Bass Tuning		
141	G G d d g g	Sonic Youth ("Tunic")

How To Tune to an Alternate Tuning

For the uninitiated, retuning the guitar to an alternate tuning can be an unsettling experience. The following chart provides several examples of what must change from standard tuning (E A d g b e′) to arrive at an alternate tuning.

If you have significant problems arriving at an alternate tuning by ear, consider using a chromatic electronic tuner. A chromatic model, as opposed to a standard-tuning-only model (with only the notes E-A-D-G-B-E), will signal when you have arrived at the desired pitch, plus let you know when it is in tune.

It also may help to write the notes of the alternate tuning you are striving for on a piece of paper next to the notes of standard tuning, as I have done in this chart. Then you will be able to see very plainly which strings must be changed to arrive at the new tuning.

Standard	Change	DAdgad′
e′	down	d′
b	down	a
g	--------	g
d	--------	d
A	--------	A
E	down	D

Standard	Change	CGcgc′e′
e′	--------	e′
b	up	c′
g	--------	g
d	down	c
A	down	G
E	down	C

Standard	Change	DGdgbd′
e′	down	d′
b	--------	b
g	--------	g
d	--------	d
A	down	G
E	down	D

Standard	Change	EEeebe′
e′	--------	e′
b	--------	b′
g	down	e
d	up	e
A	down	E
E	--------	E

Order Form

	Catalog Number	Price**
• **VIDEO INSTRUCTION**		
Fingerstyle Guitar Video (Beginning to Intermediate Levels)	V-131	$14.95
Fingerstyle Solo Guitar Video (Intermediate and Higher Levels)	V-132	$14.95
Fingerstyle Christmas Guitar, Vol.1 Video (Beginning to Upper Intermediate Levels)	V-221	$14.95
Fingerstyle Christmas Guitar, Vol. 2 Video (Lower Intermediate to Advanced Levels)	V-222	$14.95
• **TRANSCRIPTION AND INSTRUCTION BOOKS; BOOKS WITH RECORDINGS; RECORDINGS**		
Alternate Tunings Picture Chords	AM 8044	$18.95
The Complete Book of Alternate Tunings	AM 7044	$16.95
Art of Contemporary Travis Picking (book & cassette)	AM 1044	$18.95
Art of Solo Fingerpicking (book & cassette)	AM 2044	$19.95
Fingerstyle Wizard--The Wizard of Oz for Solo Guitar (book & CD)	WB 801	$19.95
Paul Simon Transcribed (book)	AM 4044	$19.95
Fingerstyle Noël (book & CD)	AM 6044BK	$19.95
Yuletide Guitar (CD)	AM 6044CD	$12.95
Yuletide Guitar (Cassette)	AM 6044CS	$ 7.95
The Music of Leo Kottke (book & cassette)	T 301	$19.95
Leo Kottke Transcribed (book & cassette)	T 302	$19.95
The Acoustic Guitar of Martin Simpson (book)	AM 5044	$17.95
The Music of Mark Hanson: Standard & Drop-D Tunings (book & cassette)	T 201	$17.95
• **"GUITAR CASE" SERIES**		
Beginning Slide Guitar (book)	MS 020	$ 5.95
12-String Guitar Guide (book)	MS 030	$ 5.95
Acoustic Jam Trax (All styles: Blues, Folk, Country, Rock, Funk; book & cassette)	MS 040	$ 9.95
Acoustic Rock Jam Trax (Acoustic Rock; book & cassette)	MS 050	$ 9.95
Acoustic Blues Jam Trax (Acoustic Blues; book & cassette)	MS 060	$ 9.95
• **FINGERSTYLE COMPACT DISCS • CASSETTES • BOTTLENECK SLIDES • OTHER MERCHANDISE**	Catalog Upon Request	

Catalog No.	Product	Quantity x	Unit Price =	Amount

SUBTOTAL $_____

SHIPPING AND HANDLING: (See chart below) $_____

California State Sales Tax (based on Subtotal from above). California residents only. $_____

Continental USA: Add $2.50 for UPS 3-Day Select. $_____

TOTAL: $_____

**Prices subject to change without notice. If not more than $5.00 extra, ship it anyway and bill me (X)_____ .

TO ORDER: Visit Your Local Music Retailer, or (In the USA) Call 1-800-313-4406, or

Call (503) 699-1814, Fax (503) 699-1813, or send VISA/MC/MONEY ORDER/CHECK (US$ drawn on a US bank), payable to

Accent On Music, D-8044, 19363 Willamette Dr. #252, West Linn, OR 97068 USA. (E-Mail Address: accentm@teleport.com)

Refund (excluding S/H) within 30 days only. Returned items must be in original condition.

Name_____

Street Address_____

_____ Business____ Residence____

City_____State/Prov._____ZIP_____

Country_____E-Mail_____

Telephone: Day (_____)_____Eve (_____)_____

VISA/MC # ___ ___ ___ ___ - ___ ___ ___ ___ - ___ ___ ___ ___ - ___

___ ___ ___ ___ Expiration Date ___ ___ ___ ___

Signature_____

Shipping & Handling Chart
Most of our orders are shipped within 24 hours of receipt.

	USA (UPS) & Canada(Air)	Europe (Airmail)	Far East Africa(Air)
$24.00 and under, add	$5.50	$10.00	$13.00
$24.01 to $50.00, add	$6.50	$16.00	$20.00
$50.01 to $100.00, add	$8.50	$22.00	$30.00
$100.01 to $140.00, add	$9.50	$28.00	$36.00
$140.01 to $200.00, add	$10.50	$35.00	$48.00
$200.00 and over, please call 503-699-1814			

Continental USA: Add $2.50 for UPS 3-Day Select.

To Contact Accent On Music, Call 1-800-313-4406 (Domestic USA Orders Only)
International Orders and Information, call: (503) 699-1814; Fax (503) 699-1813; E-Mail: accentm@teleport.com

Other Publications By Mark Hanson and Accent On Music

The Complete Book of Alternate Tunings
Fingerstyle Guitar Video (Beginning Through Intermediate)
Fingerstyle Solo Guitar Video (Intermediate Through Advanced)
The Art of Contemporary Travis Picking
The Art of Solo Fingerpicking
Fingerstyle Wizard (Wizard of Oz for Solo Guitar)
Fingerstyle Noël (Christmas Arrangements for Solo Guitar)
Yuletide Guitar (Solo Guitar Christmas CD and Cassette)
Fingerstyle Christmas Video Vol. 1 (Beg. to Upper Int.)
Fingerstyle Christmas Video Vol. 2 (Int. to Adv.)
The Acoustic Guitar of Martin Simpson
The Music of Leo Kottke
Leo Kottke Transcribed
Paul Simon Transcribed
Beginning Slide Guitar
12-String Guitar Guide
Acoustic Jam Trax
Acoustic Blues Jam Trax
Acoustic Rock Jam Trax

Acknowledgements

My first thank you goes to the many great artists who have spent time twirling their tuning machines and twisting their fingers, inventing the tunings and chords found in this book. Thanks also go to the following important people for helping to get this project off the ground: my wife, Greta Pedersen, and my family; Chris Ledgerwood for another masterful cover design; Dave McCumiskey and the staff at Music Sales Corporation, for unending support; computer gurus Patrick Mahoney, Carl Anderson, and Ken Larson; Toni Mazza at Vicks Lithograph in New York; Lake Oswego, Ore., photographers Dan Poush and Jon Pedersen; K. C. Wait of Pioneer Music in Portland, Ore., for providing the guitar; my friends at Gryphon Stringed Instruments in Palo Alto, Calif., for a steady stream of ideas; and, as always, to former *Frets* Magazine cohorts Phil Hood and Jim Hatlo for their help in making it all possible.

--Mark Hanson

About the Author

Mark Hanson is a well-known educator in the acoustic guitar field. He owns and operates Accent On Music, which publishes his numerous guitar instruction manuals and recordings. He also is a regular contributor to several guitar magazines, including *Acoustic Guitar* and *Fingerstyle Guitar.* In his days as a journalist at *Frets* Magazine in the 1980s, Mark interviewed such music industry heavyweights as James Taylor, David Crosby, Larry Carlton, Jorma Kaukonen, Leo Kottke, and Alex deGrassi. Mark currently lives with his family near Portland, Ore., and travels regularly presenting concerts and conducting guitar workshops. His first solo guitar recording, *Yuletide Guitar*, was released in 1995.